FOURTH EDITION

What Color Is Your Parachute?
JOB-HUNTER'S WORKBOOK

A Companion to the Best-Selling
Job-Hunting Book in the World

RICHARD N. BOLLES

TEN SPEED PRESS
Berkeley

People often say that this or that person has not yet found himself. But the self is not something one finds, it is something one creates.

—THOMAS SZASZ

Find what makes your heart sing and create your own music.

—MAC ANDERSON

When your heart speaks, take good notes.

—JUDITH CAMPBELL

Knowing yourself is the beginning of all wisdom.

—ARISTOTLE

Why Do You Need to Know Who You Are?

You could be doing this workbook for a number of reasons. They include:

1. You're trying to find out more about who you are, just for the fun of it. Fun? Well, why shouldn't it be? It's *you* that you're doing this homework on: what more fascinating exploration could you possibly imagine? You've got talent, no doubt about that. (Everyone has, even if they don't know what it is . . . yet.) Finding out just what your specific gifts are should be lots of fun. It all depends on the attitude you bring to it. If you think of it as a task, it will be; if you think it will be fun, it will be.

2. You're trying to make a major decision in your life: what major to pursue in college, what career to choose for your first time out of the gate into the world of work, or what career to change to, if you've been in the world of work for some time, and your present one is boring the life out of you. Knowing the answer to "Who am I?" will help tremendously with any of these decisions. Because "who am I?" involves— among other things—making a list of what you know, and what you can do. If we are in mid-life, often we can put together a new career just using what we already know, and what we already can do; we don't necessarily have to go back for three or four years of retraining. I'm not talking here about radical career changes, like *from salesperson to doctor*, or *from old-fashioned warehouse management to the mastering of CATIA systems*. For such, you obviously need additional training. But until you know who you are, you don't know what you need, or what enchants you.

3. You're at a crisis point in your life: divorce, death, the ending of some long-term job, the acquiring of a new disability in your life due to accident, disease, or war. Martin Luther King, Jr., called these *interruptions* to our life. "*The major problem of life,*" he said, "*is learning how to handle the costly interruptions. The door that slams shut, the plan that got sidetracked, the marriage that failed. Or that lovely poem that didn't get written because someone knocked on the door.*" He saw them, and so should we, as opportunities. To pause. To think. To assess where we really want to go from here, with our lives. If you begin with answering the question, "Who am I?" before you set out on your new journey, it makes all the difference in the world. You may actually trip over the answer to the most fascinating question you can ask: why are *you* here on earth, and what is your mission in life?

4. Lastly, maybe the reason you're doing this inventory of yourself *now* is because you're in some class or group, and the instructor decided everyone in the class should work through this workbook. In other words, it wasn't your choice. You had nothing to say about it.

Okay, use the opportunity. Make this time of your life a hunt for a deeper life. A life you're prouder of. A victorious life.

Dream a little. Dream a lot. One of the saddest lines in the world is, "Oh come now—be realistic." The best parts of this world were not fashioned by those who were realistic. They were fashioned by those who dared to look hard at their wishes and then gave them horses to ride.

What Language Shall We Use to Describe Who You Are?

What language do we want to use, to describe who you are? I'm not referring to languages such as English, French, or Chinese here; I'm thinking of *life languages.* There are three of them, because there are three worlds we live in, during our lifetime: the world of education, then the world of work, and finally the world of leisure or retirement:

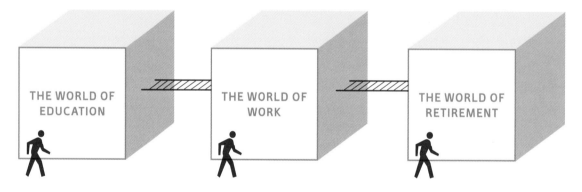

In each of these worlds, we can—and do—use different language. For example, in the world of education our language is about ourselves as *student.* In the world of work our language is about ourselves as *worker.* And in the world of leisure our language is about ourselves as *player.* So, the first decision we have to make, once we decide to inventory and describe who we are, is, "In what language shall we describe ourselves—the language of student, the language of worker, or the language of player?"

In this workbook, and elsewhere, we have opted for the language describing you as worker. Why? Well, it is *relatively* easy to get into the world of learning—though in terms of college, it is getting harder; and it is relatively easy to get into the world of leisure. What is difficult is getting into the world of work, or getting back into the world of work. For this, you need the most time, the best tools, the hardest thinking, and the strongest preparation. It is best, then, to describe yourself to yourself in the language of *work.* In this workbook, this is what we shall do. And so, we begin.

You are about to enter a new world.

The world of Card Sorts.

Get out your scissors.

Page 5 will explain.

IDEAS	PEOPLE	OBJECTS, MACHINES
MONEY	SYMBOLS, EQUATIONS	COMPUTERS, ELECTRONICS, GAMES
GRAPHICS	WORDS	MUSIC
COLOR	LIGHT	SOUND
SPACES, SPACE	WATER	PAPER
WOOD	PLANTS, TREES	FOOD, CROPS, GRAINS
EARTH, MATERIALS, MINERALS	ANIMALS	CLOTHES

I Am a Person Who . . .

You begin by stripping yourself of any job-title. You have to stop answering, *"Who are you?"* with, "Oh, I'm a construction worker, or salesperson, or designer, or writer, or whatever." That locks you into the past. You launch yourself into the future by instead answering, *"Who are you?"* with: *"I am a person who . . ."*

"I am a person who . . . has had these experiences." *"I am a person who . . .* is skilled at doing this or that." *"I am a person who . . .* knows a lot about this or that." *"I am a person who . . .* is unusual in this way or that."

I Am a Person Who . . . Is an Artist

Begin by thinking about the general subject of your *work*. How would you describe *work*? A way to make money, sure. But *if* it's more than that, then your work is how you express yourself and who you are. And *if given a choice*, whatever work you choose ends up being **the expression of your own personality, working through some** *medium*.[1] That's obvious in the case of an artist. But it's true of every man and every woman who chooses their work. You are an artist in some sense or another, so **a career choice is essentially the choice of what** *medium* **you prefer, to express who you are.**

For the artist, the medium may be oils on canvas, or drama, or poetry, or marble, or the stage. For the rest of us, there are other mediums through which we express our personality and uniqueness.

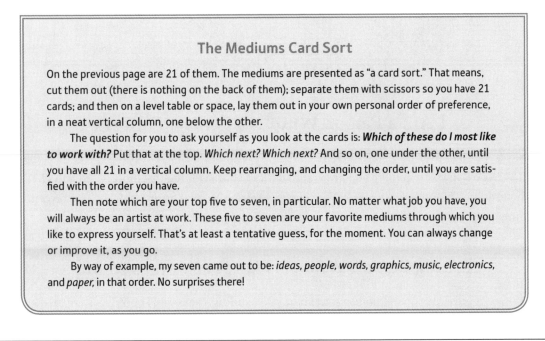

The Mediums Card Sort

On the previous page are 21 of them. The mediums are presented as "a card sort." That means, cut them out (there is nothing on the back of them); separate them with scissors so you have 21 cards; and then on a level table or space, lay them out in your own personal order of preference, in a neat vertical column, one below the other.

The question for you to ask yourself as you look at the cards is: *Which of these do I most like to work with?* Put that at the top. *Which next? Which next?* And so on, one under the other, until you have all 21 in a vertical column. Keep rearranging, and changing the order, until you are satisfied with the order you have.

Then note which are your top five to seven, in particular. No matter what job you have, you will always be an artist at work. These five to seven are your favorite mediums through which you like to express yourself. That's at least a tentative guess, for the moment. You can always change or improve it, as you go.

By way of example, my seven came out to be: *ideas, people, words, graphics, music, electronics,* and *paper,* in that order. No surprises there!

---

1. I always like to give credit for ideas. This idea was first formulated almost a century ago, by an engineer named John Mills at a company called Western Electric, 1918.

I Am a Person Who ... *Is Like a Flower*

Before you put the cards back in a stack, you want to jot down those top favorites, of course. On pages 8–9 you'll find the graphic you are going to fill in to answer the question "Who Am I?" We call the graphic *The Flower Diagram*, or *The Flower Exercise*. To start, write your top five favorite mediums from the Card Sort onto the Favorite Knowledges petal.

I Am a Person Who ... *Has Seven Sides to Me*

This flower representation of *You* has *seven* petals (including the center) because there are seven sides to You, or seven ways of thinking about yourself.

Seven Ways of Describing Who You Are

1. You can describe *who you are* in terms of **what you know**—and what your *favorite* knowledges or fields of interest are, that you have stored in your head (or heart).

2. Or you can describe *who you are* in terms of **the kinds of people** you most prefer to *work with*, and/or the kinds of people—age span, problems, handicaps, geographical location, etc.—you would most like to *help* or serve.

3. Or you can describe *who you are* in terms of **what you can do**, and what your *favorite* functional/transferable skills are.

4. Or you can describe *who you are* in terms of your favorite **working conditions**—indoors/outdoors, small company/large company, tight ship/loose ship,[2] windows/no windows, etc.—because they enable you to work at your top form, and greatest effectiveness.

5. Or you can describe *who you are* in terms of **your preferred salary, level, and responsibility**—working by yourself, or as a member of a team, or supervising others, or running the show—that you feel most fitted for, by experience, temperament, and appetite.

6. Or you can describe *who you are* in terms of **your preferred geographical location**—here or abroad, warm/cold, north/south, east/west, mountains/coast, urban/suburban/rural/rustic—where you'd be happiest, do your best work, and would most love to live.

7. Or you can describe *who you are* in terms of **your goals or sense of mission and purpose** for your life. Alternatively, or in addition, you can get more particular and describe the goals or mission you want *the organization* to have, where you decide to work.

I Am a Person Who . . . *Is All These Things*

You could choose just one, two, or three of these sides of yourself—let us say, "what you know," "what you can do," and "preferred salary"—as your guide to defining who you are, in the language of work.

But what the Flower Diagram does is describe who you are in *all seven* ways, joined together on one page, in one graphic. After all, you are not just one of these things; you are *all* of these things. The Flower Diagram is a complete, not partial, picture of *You*.

So please fill in your Flower. *And try to keep it a joy rather than a duty.*

---

2. "Tight ship": you clock in and clock out, work under strict conditions; "loose ship": you have greater leeway about when you come in, or go home, they want your creativity above all else, and there is no time clock or tight supervision of your day.

The Flower

"That One Piece of Paper"

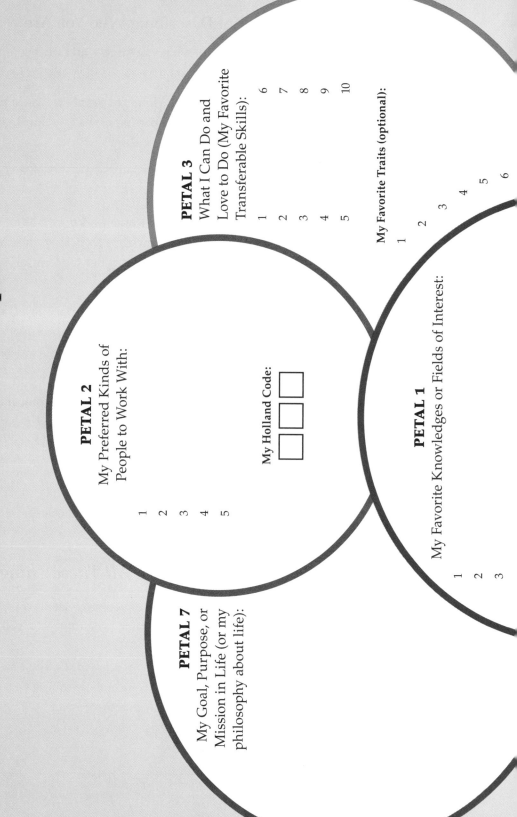

PETAL 2

My Preferred Kinds of
People to Work With:

1
2
3
4
5

My Holland Code: ☐ ☐ ☐ ☐

PETAL 3

What I Can Do and
Love to Do (My Favorite
Transferable Skills):

1   6
2   7
3   8
4   9
5   10

My Favorite Traits (optional):

1   2   3   4   5   6

PETAL 1

My Favorite Knowledges or Fields of Interest:

1
2
3

PETAL 7

My Goal, Purpose, or
Mission in Life (or my
philosophy about life):

PETAL 4

My Favorite Working
Conditions:

1

2

3

4

5

Favorite Mediums:

1

2

3

4

5

PETAL 5

My Preferred Salary Range:

Level of Responsibility I'd Like:

Other Rewards Hoped For:

4

5

PETAL 6

My Preferred Place(s) to
Live (sooner or later):

1

2

3

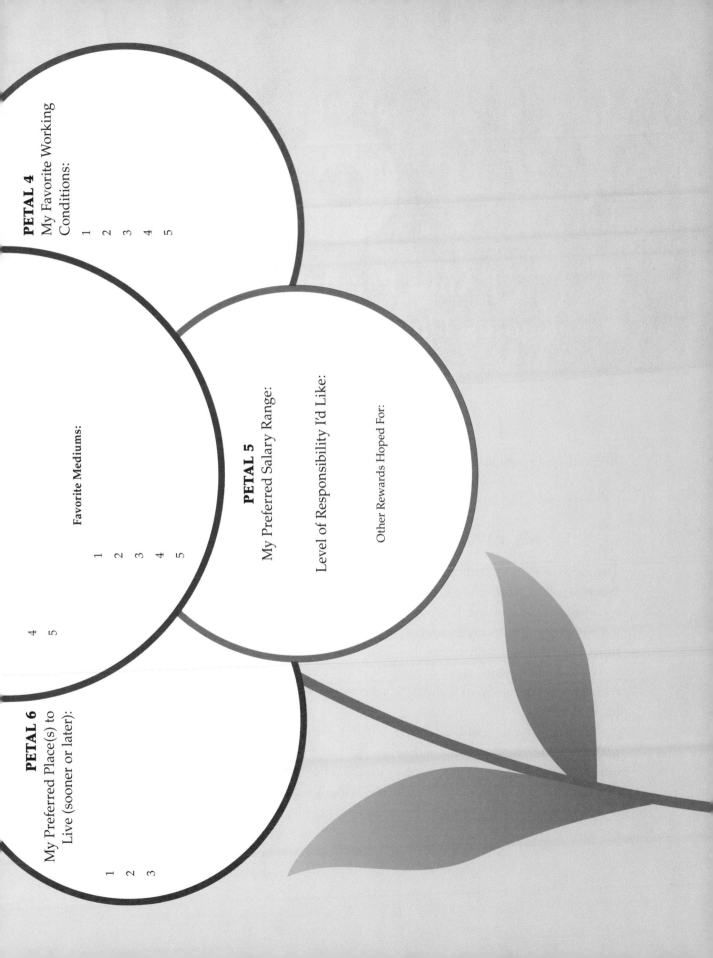

PETAL 1

I Am a Person Who . . .
Knows These Particular Things

And *loves* using that knowledge. Or knowledges. Or "know hows." (Call it what you will.)

FIRST PETAL:
My Favorite Knowledges or Fields of Interest

There are three things traditionally called skills: *functions*, *also known as transferable skills;* **knowledges**; and **traits.** As a general rule throughout this homework, *knowledges are nouns, traits are adjectives or adverbs, and transferable skills are verbs.* If it helps knowing that, great; if not, forget it. Our overarching principle always is: if a generalization or bunch of categories help you, use them. But if they just confuse you, then ignore them!!! Please!

On this Knowledges "petal" *(actually the central part of the Flower Diagram)* you will eventually write your final results: your Favorite Knowledges/Fields of Interest, prioritized in their order of importance to you.

Prior to that, you need here, as you will with each petal, a worksheet. A worksheet is **a gathering place,** for the results of the exercises you do, but also for every bright idea, every hunch, every remembered dream, every intuition that occurs to you as you are working on that petal. Jot down *everything*. A worksheet is like **a fisherman's net**, where you want to cast it into the sea in order to capture the largest haul possible, and then sort out the best of your catch, later.

This worksheet can look sloppy, unorganized, and messy. That's okay. Who cares? Only the final Flower petal is supposed to look organized.

This is an important petal—very important—so to unearth your favorite knowledges or fields of interest, four exercises are usually needed. We begin with:

1. What You Know About Each of Your Favorite Mediums That Enables You to Work Better in That Medium

Here, jot down your favorite mediums that you like to work with or in—from the Card Sort, remember? My seven, you will recall, were, in order: *ideas, people, words, graphics, music, electronics, and paper.* Put yours down, now (not mine), at the top of the worksheet, in order of your personal favorites. Then, in section 1, jot down anything you *know* about any medium of yours, **that enables you to work better in that medium.** Think of *what you know* that someone brand new to that medium wouldn't know.

If, for example, a favorite medium for you is **computers**, then the question is: what do you know, that someone brand new to the medium wouldn't know? Maybe you know the Mac operating system really well. Put down: *Mac OS X 10.7.* Maybe you know how to repair a computer. Put down: *computer repair.* Maybe you know how to use the computer to do graphic design. Put down: *digital graphic design.* Maybe you know how to write source code. Put down: *source code.* Maybe you know the way to write mobile apps for iTunes (or Android). Put down: *how to write mobile apps.* Any things you know that enable you to work better in the medium called *computers,* are Knowledges.

WORKSHEET

Notes About My Favorite Knowledges
My Favorite Mediums a. b. c. d. e. f. g.
1. What You Know About Each of Your Favorite Mediums That Enables You to Work Better in That Medium
2. What You Know from Your Previous Jobs

WORKSHEET

Notes About My Favorite Knowledges
3. What You Know About, Outside of Work
4. What Fields, Careers, or Industries Sound Interesting to You
Any Other Hunches, Bright Ideas, Great Ideas, etc.

Again, if a preferred medium of yours here is **games**, then jot down any knowledge you have about games, or a particular game, *that enables you to work better in that medium.* For example, it could be: *how to win at Mass Effect 3,* or perhaps *how to play multiplayer videogames,* or maybe, *the Minimax Theorem,* or perhaps *theory of zero-sum games,* or the *Xbox 360,* or even *how to play MMORPGs like World of Warcraft, etc.* Any knowledge or "know how" you have about that medium, or anything in that medium, that enables you to work more confidently in that medium, that someone new to the medium wouldn't know, should be put down here.

As you look at a favorite medium of yours, maybe you will come up empty. Can't think of a single thing that helps you work better in that medium. Well, you're probably kidding yourself; but let's let that go, for the time being. Just give this exercise your best shot. It takes time, of course, because it requires *thinking.* You may be sitting there, staring at the walls for a spell, as the sweat stands out upon your brow. But eventually, an idea will break out.

Thinking in terms of whatever *pictures* come to your mind, rather than just searching for *words,* sometimes helps a lot.

There is no penalty for coming up empty. Only for not trying at all.

2. What You Know from Your Previous Jobs

If you've been out there in the world of work for any time already, you've probably learned a lot of things that you now just take for granted. "*Of course I know* that!" But such knowledges may be important, down the line. So, list them!

Things like: *bookkeeping, handling applications, credit collection of overdue accounts, hiring, international business, management, marketing, sales, merchandizing, packaging, policy development, problem solving, troubleshooting, public speaking, recruiting, conference planning, systems analysis, the culture of other countries, other languages, government contract procedures,* and so on.

To be thorough here, jot down a list of all the jobs you have ever held, and then *for each job* jot down anything you learned there. For example: "Worked in a warehouse; learned *how to use a forklift and crane, inventory control, logistics automation software, Warehouse Management systems, JIT (just in time) techniques, teamwork principles,* and *how to supervise employees.*"

Or, again, "Worked at McDonald's: learned *how to prepare and serve food, how to wait on customers, how to make change, how to deal with complaints, how to train new employees, etc.*"

Do this with all the jobs you have ever held: where you worked, what you learned there. Then look over everything you've written in *this* exercise, and decide which are your favorite knowledges or interests, that you're glad you picked up. Jot them down on your worksheet, in the space provided for this exercise.

3. What You Know About, Outside of Work

Also jot down knowledges you've picked up outside of work, such as: *antiques, gardening, cooking, budgeting, decorating, photography, crafts, spirituality, sports, camping, travel, repairing things, flea markets, scrapbooking, sewing, art appreciation at museums, how to run or work in a volunteer organization,* and so on.

a. Also think of anything you learned or are learning in high school (or college) that you prize knowing today: *keyboarding? Chinese? accounting? geography?* What? Jot it all down.

b. Think of anything you learned at training seminars, workshops, conferences, and so on, possibly in connection with a job you had at the time. Jot it all down.

c. Think of anything you studied at home, via online courses, mobile apps, tape programs (likely played in your car while commuting), PBS television programs, etc. Jot it all down.

d. Think of anything you learned out there in the world, such as *how to assemble a flash mob, how to organize a protest, how to fundraise for a particular cause, how to run a marathon, how to repair a toilet,* etc. Jot it all down, in the space provided for this exercise on your worksheet.

4. What Fields, Careers, or Industries Sound Interesting to You

If you want to pick some career or field from a list of them all, it helps if you start broadly, and then drill down.

Broadly speaking, then, the world out there consists of the following four arenas: *agriculture, manufacturing, information,* or *services.* Any ideas about which of these four is most attractive to you? If so, jot it down, in the space provided for this exercise on your worksheet.

In order to drill down further than that, your best bet is the government's O*Net Online, assuming you have a computer or tablet (**www.onetonline.org**; *note that is .org, not .com*).

To begin with, this site has various lists of **career clusters** or **industries** or **job families.** Below is a mashup of these. Please read this list over, and check off any of these that you want to explore further *(multiple choice preferred, here, in order to have alternatives and therefore Hope)*:

❏ Accommodation and Food Services

❏ Administrative and Support Services

❏ Agriculture, Food, and Natural Resources

❏ Architecture, Engineering, and Construction

❏ Arts, Audio/Video Technology, and Communications

❏ Business, Operations, Management, and Administration

❏ Community and Social Service

❏ Computer and Mathematical

❏ Design, Entertainment, Sports, and Media

- ❏ Distribution and Logistics
- ❏ Education, Training, and Library
- ❏ Entertainment and Recreation
- ❏ Farming, Forestry, Fishing, and Hunting
- ❏ Finance and Insurance
- ❏ Food Preparation and Serving
- ❏ Government and Public Administration
- ❏ Green Industries or Jobs
- ❏ Health Care, Health Science, and Social Assistance
- ❏ Hospitality and Tourism
- ❏ Human Services
- ❏ Information and Information Technology
- ❏ Law, Public Safety, Corrections, and Security
- ❏ Life, Physical, and Social Sciences
- ❏ Manufacturing
- ❏ Management of Companies and Enterprises
- ❏ Marketing, Sales, and Service
- ❏ Military Related
- ❏ Mining, Quarrying, and Oil and Gas Extraction
- ❏ Personal Care and Service
- ❏ Production
- ❏ Professional, Scientific, and Technical Services
- ❏ Protective Services
- ❏ Real Estate, Rental, and Leasing
- ❏ Religion, Faith, and Related
- ❏ Retail Trade, Sales, and Related
- ❏ Science, Technology, Engineering, and Mathematics
- ❏ Self-Employment
- ❏ Transportation, Warehousing, and Material Moving
- ❏ Utilities

Now, the nice thing about O*Net Online is that once you have chosen anything on the list above, the site has drop-down menus which allow you to go deeper into each *career cluster, industry,* or *job family* that you have checked off. It drills down to **career pathways**, and then drills down further to **individual occupations**, and then drills down still further to **tasks, tools, technologies, knowledges, skills, abilities, work activities, education, interests, work styles, work values, related occupations,** and **salary.**

The only limitation here, is that O*Net *only does this for about 974 occupations.* Its predecessor, the D.O.T., had 12,741 occupations.[3] So, this does not offer a complete map of the job-market by any means.

And even for those occupations that are listed in O*Net, remember: jobs, industries, and careers are mortal: they are born, they grow, they flourish, they mature, then decline and ultimately die. Sometimes it takes centuries, sometimes merely decades, sometimes even sooner than that. But, eventually, most jobs, industries, and careers are mortal. So, always have a plan b.

---

3. By the way, if you want to use or visit the D.O.T. it's now online at www.occupationalinfo.org, and can be downloaded to your computer.

Okay, now you're done with the worksheet for this petal. What next? Well, sort them. Sort everything—everything—you have on that worksheet into one of the following four bins (well, you can forget bin #4, if you'd rather):

Your Favorite Subjects Matrix

HIGH

3. Subjects for Which You Have Little Enthusiasm but in Which You Have Lots of Expertise

1. Subjects for Which You Have Lots of Enthusiasm and in Which You Have Lots of Expertise BINGO!

4. Subjects for Which You Have Little Enthusiasm and in Which you Have Little Expertise

2. Subjects for Which You Have Lots of Enthusiasm but in Which You Have Little Expertise

NO

EXPERTISE

LOW ⟵——— ENTHUSIASM ———⟶ HIGH

Copy the top four or five results from bin #1 and maybe, maybe, an item from bin #2, on to your Favorite Knowledges or Fields of Interest petal, found on pages 8–9.

Now you're ready to move on, to consider another side of Who You Are.

PETAL 2

I Am a Person Who . . .
Has These Favorite Kinds of People

SECOND PETAL:
My Preferred Kinds of People to Work With

The people we surround ourselves with, at play or at work, are either energy drainers or energy creators. They either drag us down, and keep us from being our most effective, or they lift us up and help us to be at our best, and perform at our greatest effectiveness. We'll get into that, in a minute.

Also, "people-environments" are another way of describing jobs or careers. So, let us begin with the following chart.

And, by the way, you can fill it out alone, or in company with up to five other job-hunters (recommended, because it's a lot more fun to see how other people are bugged by the same kinds of people that you are).

My Favorite People Petal

Goal in Filling Out This Petal: To avoid past bad experiences with people at work or play, since who (*whom?*) you surround yourself with can either make the day delightful, or ruin it altogether.

What You Are Looking For: (1) A better picture in your mind of what kind of people surrounding you at play or work will enable you to operate at your highest and most effective level. (2) If a medium you chose during the Card Sort was "people," then this helps to describe what people you would most like to serve or help: defined by age, problems, geography, and so forth.

Form of the Entries on Your Petal: They can be adjectives describing different kinds of people ("kind," "patient") or they can be types of people, as in the "Holland Code" or "Myers-Briggs" typologies (see pages 27 and 33).

Example of a Good Petal: (1) *Kind, generous, understanding, fun, smart.* (2) *The unemployed, people struggling with their faith, worldwide, all ages. Holland code: IAS.*

Example of a Bad Petal: *People in trouble, young, smart, in urban settings. RCI.*

Why Bad: It doesn't distinguish between (1) people surrounding me at work and (2) people I want to help or serve. It lumps both together. Not much help. Too vague.

MY FAVORITE PEOPLE CHART

Column 1	Column 2
Places I Have Worked Thus Far in My Life	Kinds of People There Who Drove Me Nuts (from the places listed in the first column) (No names, but describe *what* about them drove you nuts; e.g., *bossy, always pestering me with their personal problems, always left early before job was done, etc.* List these in any order; it doesn't matter—at least in *this* column . . .)

MY FAVORITE PEOPLE CHART

Column 3	Column 4
Kinds of People I'd Prefer Not to Have to Work With, In Order, Starting with the Worst	Kinds of People I'd Most Like to Work With, in Order of Preference
(This is now a ranking of the items in the second column, in exact order of: which is worse? next? etc. Use the Prioritizing Grid, on the following page, to do this.)	(The opposite of those qualities in the third column, in the same order.)
1a.	1b.
2a.	2b.
3a.	3b.
4a.	4b.
5a.	5b.

Start, of course, by filling in the first column in the Chart, and then the second. This will bring you to the third column, and here you're gonna need some help. How do you look back at that stuff in the second column, and prioritize it? Well, you use:

The Prioritizing Grid

I give you my Prioritizing Grid. It asks you to decide between just two items at a time.

Instructions for Using the Prioritizing Grid

Section A: Write down, in any order, the factors you listed in the second column of the Chart. This grid will accommodate up to ten factors. If you originally listed more than ten, take a guess at which ten factors you disliked the most, and list *those ten*.

Section B: Compare just two items at a time. Begin with that little tiny box to the left of factor #1 and factor #2, in which you will see the tiny numbers 1 and 2. The numbers are clearly short-hand for those factors written out in Section A. The question you would frame for yourself, here, would be as follows: which of these two factors do I dislike the most? Then, in that little tiny box you circle either the tiny number 1 or 2, depending on which factor you dislike the most.

In similar manner you work your way down the little boxes *nearest* Section A, which as you can see lie in a diagonal running from northwest to southeast. The next little tiny box has the tiny numbers 2 and 3 in it. Same question, except now it's between factor #2 versus factor #3. Circle the appropriate number in that tiny box. Why *diagonal*, rather than just straight across horizontally or straight down, vertically? Because you can get into a knee-jerk reaction if you do it that way (*"Well, I checked factor #5 each time so far, so I guess I should check factor #5 this next time, too."*) Diagonal defeats knee-jerk reactions.

So, work your way on down in that diagonal direction. When you've reached the little box at the bottom of that first diagonal (containing the little numbers 9 and 10), go back up to the top and work down the next diagonal (beginning with the little box containing 1 and 3; then the little box containing 2 and 4; then the one containing 3 and 5, etc.

When you've reached the box at the bottom of *that* diagonal direction, go back up to the top, and work down the next diagonal (the little box containing 1 and 4, then the box containing 2 and 5, and so on, down to the box containing 7 and 10).

Back up to the top to the next diagonal, the box containing 1 and 5, then the box containing 2 and 6, and so on. Keep this up until you've made a decision about every little box (the final one being 1 versus 10).

Section C: The bottom of the grid has three rows to it, as you can see. The first row is already filled in for you: it's the numbers of the factors in Section A. The second row, just below that, asks how many times each number got circled in *all* of the little tiny boxes. Let's say tiny number 1 got circled 7 times. In the row right beneath the number 1 in the first row of Section C, you enter the

OUR PRIORITIZING GRID FOR 10 ITEMS OR LESS

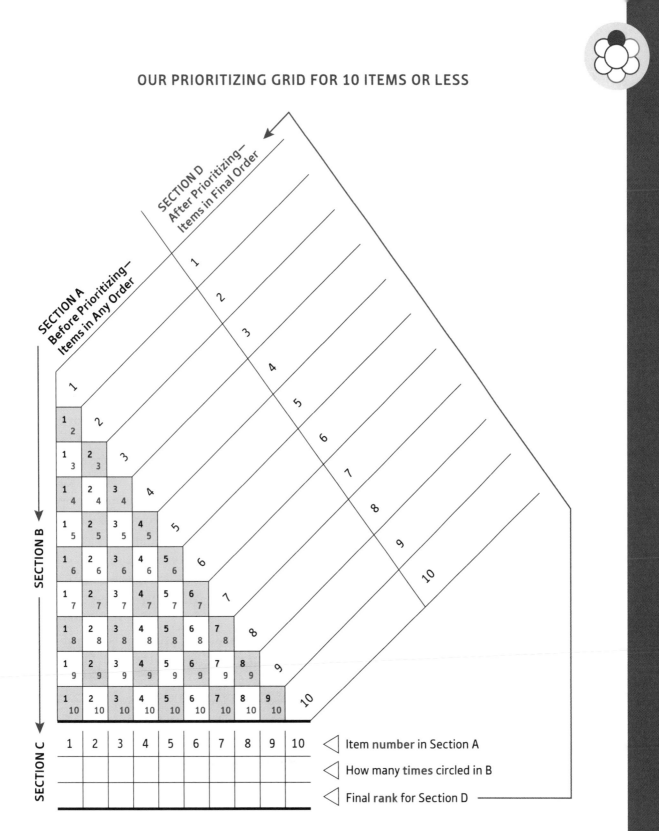

SECTION D
After Prioritizing—
Items in Final Order

SECTION A
Before Prioritizing—
Items in Any Order

SECTION B

SECTION C

◁ Item number in Section A

◁ How many times circled in B

◁ Final rank for Section D

number 7. Next, count how many times item 2 got circled; let's say it was one time; put the number 1 right below #2. Continue up through item 10.

Look now at the numbers in that second row. If no number is repeated in that second row of Section C, great! Most likely you'll find a tie. That means two items got circled the same number of times—let's say 2 and 10. How do you resolve the tie? Well, you look back at Section B, to find the little tiny box that had 2 and 10 in it, and see which of those two you circled there; let's say it was 2. Well then, in that second row, give #2 an extra half point. Now its "count" is $1^1/_2$. Leave #10 as it is (count just 1). Do this with each two-way tie.

What do you do if you have a three-way tie—three items each got circled the same number of times? This always means that you contradicted yourself somewhere along the way: one time you said *this* was more important, another time you said, no it wasn't. The only way to resolve the three-way tie is to just guess what is the proper order (for you) as to which of the three you dislike the most, which next, which next. Let's say the tie was that 3, 4, and 7 all got circled the same number of times. You dislike #7 the most, #4 next, and #3 after that. Okay, so give an extra $^3/_4$ point *(that's three-quarters of a point)* to #7, an extra $^1/_2$ point to #4, and no extra points to factor #3. Now, no two factors or items have the same count in the second line of Section C.

Go down now to the bottom row there in Section C, and now **rank** the items, according to their circle count in the second row. The factor that got circled the most, let's say it was item #6, must be given *a final rank* of 1. Therefore, write 1 in the third row, down below item #6. Let's say item #8 got the next most circles; write a 2 down below item #8. Let's say item #1 got the next most circles; write a 3 down below it, on the bottom rank line in Section C. And so on. And so forth.

Section D. Recopy the list that you randomly put down in Section A, but now here in Section D put the list in its exact order of *one you disliked the most, next most,* etc.—according to the ranking in the bottom row of Section C. In terms of our examples above, you would copy item #6 (as it was called in Section A), and put it on the very top line in Section D, because it got circled the most. You would copy item #8 (as it was called in Section A) onto the second line in Section D, because it got circled the next most times. And so on, until you've copied all ten factors in exactly the order of "dis-like-ness" (new word) this Grid revealed.

Now, what do you end up with, there in Section D? A list of your preferences, regarding people-environments: *"I would most prefer not to have to work with . . . and I next most prefer not to have to work with. . . ."* etc.

I knew you'd like an example of a finished Prioritizing Grid, which is what you have on the opposite page. Note that there is a mistake on line 3 in Section D. No matter if you make a mistake. Just cross it out and put the correct information. It's okay not to be perfect.

Now, back to the *Chart* on page 21. Copy the first five factors in Section D of the *Grid*, into the third column of the *Chart*. What you've got there, now, is a *negative* list of what you're trying to avoid. What you want is a *positive* list of what you're trying to find.

So, look at the five negative items you just put up there, in the third column of the Chart, and write *the opposite*, or something near the opposite, in the fourth column directly across from each item in the third column. By "opposite" I don't necessarily mean "the exact opposite." If one of your complaints in the third column was: "I was micromanaged, supervised every hour of my day," the opposite, in the fourth column, wouldn't necessarily be "No supervision." It might be "Limited supervision" or something like that. Your call.

Note that by first putting your *negative* list in exact order of what you **most want to avoid** (third column in the Chart), your related *positive* list (fourth column) will have its factors in the exact order of what you **most want to find** in a future job.

Now copy the top 5 on your *positive* list, on to the petal, My Preferred Kinds of People to Work With, on page 8.

Then we move on, to do the rest of the petal.

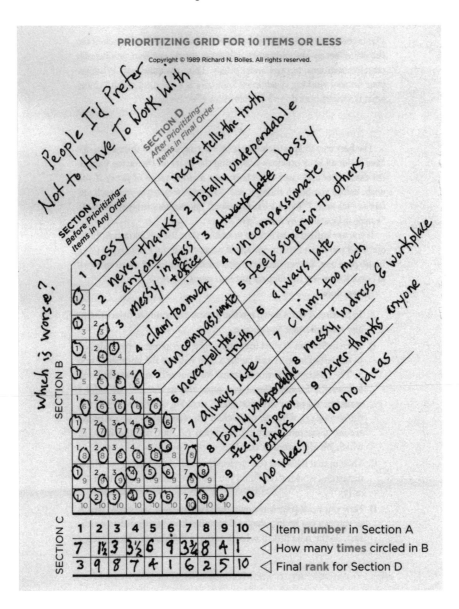

The *Party Game* Exercise

People-environments aren't just a matter of figuring out who irritates you and who doesn't. Though that is important. But, *people* are also a way of identifying careers.

That's because every career has a characteristic people-environment. Tell us what **career** interests you, and we can tell you, in general terms, what people-environment it will offer—described in terms of six factors.

Or tell us what **people-environment** you want—in terms of those same six factors—and we can tell you what careers will give you *that*. As I always like to give credit where credit is due, you should know that it was the late Dr. John L. Holland who came up with the system for doing this.[4]

Surveying the whole world out there, he said there are basically six people-environments. Let's tick them off:

1. **Realistic** People-Environment: Filled with people who prefer activities involving "the explicit, ordered, or systematic manipulation of objects, tools, machines, and animals." "Realistic," incidentally, refers to Plato's conception of "the real" as that which one can apprehend through the senses. ("Knock on wood!")

   I summarize this as: **R** = *people who like nature, or plants, or animals, or athletics, or tools and machinery, or being outdoors.*

2. **Investigative** People-Environment: Filled with people who prefer activities involving "the observation and symbolic, systematic, creative investigation of physical, biological, or cultural phenomena."

   I summarize this as: **I** = *people who are very curious, liking to investigate or analyze things, or people, or data.*

3. **Artistic** People-Environment: Filled with people who prefer activities involving "ambiguous, free, unsystematized activities and competencies to create art forms or products."

   I summarize this as: **A** = *people who are very artistic, imaginative, and innovative, and don't like time clocks.*

4. **Social** People-Environment: Filled with people who prefer activities involving "the manipulation of others to inform, train, develop, cure, or enlighten."

   I summarize this as: **S** = *people who are bent on trying to help, teach, or serve people.*

---

4. There is, incidentally, a relationship between the **people** you like to be surrounded by and your **skills** and your **values**. Most of us don't need to explore that, but if you're curious, you'll need to read John Holland's book, *Making Vocational Choices* (3rd ed., 1997). You can procure it at your local public library or (if you can afford it) by going to the Psychological Assessment Resources (PAR), Inc., website at www3.parinc.com, and entering the word "Holland" in the search engine there; or by calling 1-800-331-8378. The book is $56.00 at this writing. PAR also has John Holland's instrument, called The Self-Directed Search (or SDS, for short), for discovering what your Holland Code is. PAR lets you take the test online for a small fee ($4.95) at www.self-directed-search.com.

5. **Enterprising** People-Environment: Filled with people who prefer activities involving "the manipulation of others to attain organizational or self-interest goals."

   I summarize this as: E = people who like to start up projects or organizations, or sell things, or influence and persuade people.

6. **Conventional** People-Environment: Filled with people who prefer activities involving "the explicit, ordered, systematic manipulation of data, such as keeping records, filing materials, reproducing materials, organizing written and numerical data according to a prescribed plan, operating business and data-processing machines." "Conventional," incidentally, refers to the "values" that people in this environment usually hold— representing the central mainstream of our culture.

   I summarize this as: C = people who like detailed work, and like to complete tasks or projects.

According to John's theory, every one of us has **three** preferred people-environments, from among these six. The letters for your three preferred people-environments gives you what he called your "Holland Code." The question for you is: Which three?

Back in 1975 I invented a quick and easy way for you to find out, based on John's system. It's turned out it corresponds to the results you would get from taking the SDS, 92 percent of the time.[5] So if you want a much more certain answer, you should take the SDS. But when you're in a hurry, this is close. I call it "The Party Exercise." Here is how the exercise goes (*do it, please*).

---

5. Amusing anecdote: John was a good friend of mine, and when I first showed him this Party Exercise I had invented, I asked him what he thought of it. With a twinkle in his eye he snorted, "Huh! Probably put me out of business!" Nope, it didn't. His SDS has sold more than thirty million copies, and is the basis for many other career tests or instruments.

On the previous page is an aerial view of a room in which a party is taking place. At this party, people with the same interests have (for some reason) all gathered in the same corner of the room. And that's true for all six corners.

1. Which corner of the room would you instinctively be drawn to, as the group of people you would most enjoy being with for the longest time? (Leave aside any question of shyness, or whether you would have to actually talk to them; you could just listen.) Write the letter for that corner here: ☐

2. After fifteen minutes, everyone in the corner you chose leaves for another party cross-town, except you. Of the groups that still remain now, which corner or group would you be drawn to the most, as the people you would most enjoy being with for the longest time? Write the letter for that corner here: ☐

3. After fifteen minutes, this group too leaves for another party, except you. Of the corners, and groups, which remain now, which one would you most enjoy being with for the longest time? Write the letter for that corner here: ☐

The three letters you just chose are called your "Holland Code."[6]

Put that code here: ☐ ☐ ☐

Now, copy that code onto the petal, My Preferred Kinds of People to Work With, found on page 8. And we are done (with that petal).

Time now to move on to another side of Who You Are.

---

6. Incidentally, John always encouraged people to write down somewhere all six versions (technically called *permutations*) of your code. Thus, if your code were, say, SIA, its permutations would be: SIA, SAI, IAS, ISA, ASI, AIS. This is especially useful if you are ever going to look up careers that correspond to your code. Put "Holland codes for careers" into your favorite search engine, and you will find such sites as www.vista-cards.com/occupations.

Further, he and I worked together on this application of his system to our Daydreams: list all the things you've ever dreamed of doing. Then, to the right of each, try to *guess*—guess!—at what you think the three-letter Holland code would be for each. When done, look at each code and assign a value of 3 to any letter in the first position; assign a value of 2 to any letter in the second position; and assign a value of 1 to any letter in the third position (e.g., in the case of IAS, you'd give 3 points to "I," 2 points to "A," and 1 point to "S"). Do this for every code you've written down, then total up all the points for each letter. How many points did "R" get, how many points did "I" get, etc. Choose the top three with the most points, in order, and when you're done, you have the Holland Code of your daydreams. As John said to me, "This is the most reliable way of determining someone's code, but who would believe it, except you and me?"

PETAL 3

I Am a Person Who . . .
Can Do These Particular Things

And *loves* using these transferable skills. Or gifts. Or talents. Or abilities. (Or whatever you want to call them.)

THIRD PETAL:
What I Can Do (My Favorite Transferable Skills)

Incidentally, there is a new category floating around in the past ten years, called "soft skills." These are really just another way of speaking of people-skills or traits, and involve things like "a good work ethic," "a positive attitude," "acting as a team player," "flexibility," "working well under pressure," and "ability to learn from criticism."

You will also find some people or websites describing *categories* of transferable skills, like "action verbs," or "communication or people skills," "technical skills," "research and analytical skills," "management, supervision, and leadership skills," "clerical and administrative skills," "problem-solving and development skills," "financial skills," etc. It's a hazy science. I still prefer "skills with data, or people, or things." It's simple (so, apparently, am I).

Here, you are looking for what you may think of as the basic building-blocks of your work. So, if you're going to identify your dream job, and/or attempt a thorough career-change, you must, above all else, identify your functional, transferable skills. And while you may think you know what your best and favorite skills are, in most cases, your self-knowledge could probably use a little work.

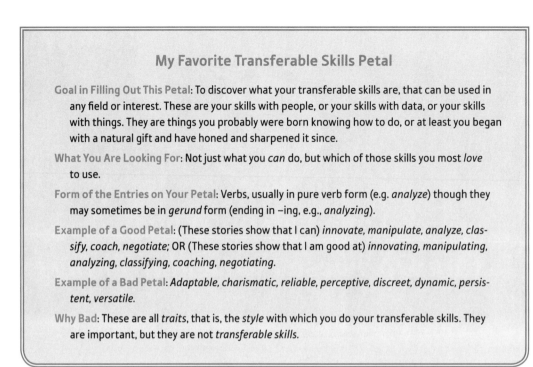

My Favorite Transferable Skills Petal

Goal in Filling Out This Petal: To discover what your transferable skills are, that can be used in any field or interest. These are your skills with people, or your skills with data, or your skills with things. They are things you probably were born knowing how to do, or at least you began with a natural gift and have honed and sharpened it since.

What You Are Looking For: Not just what you *can* do, but which of those skills you most *love* to use.

Form of the Entries on Your Petal: Verbs, usually in pure verb form (e.g. *analyze*) though they may sometimes be in *gerund* form (ending in –ing, e.g., *analyzing*).

Example of a Good Petal: (These stories show that I can) *innovate, manipulate, analyze, classify, coach, negotiate*; OR (These stories show that I am good at) *innovating, manipulating, analyzing, classifying, coaching, negotiating.*

Example of a Bad Petal: *Adaptable, charismatic, reliable, perceptive, discreet, dynamic, persistent, versatile.*

Why Bad: These are all *traits*, that is, the *style* with which you do your transferable skills. They are important, but they are not *transferable skills*.

A weekend should do it! In a weekend, you can inventory your *past* sufficiently so that you have a good picture of the *kind* of work you would love to be doing *in the future*. (*You can, of course, stretch the inventory over a number of weeks, maybe doing an hour or two one night a week, if you prefer. It's up to you as to how fast you do it.*)

A Crash Course on "Transferable Skills"

Many people just "freeze" when they hear the word "skills."

It begins with high school job-hunters: "I haven't really got any skills," they say.

It continues with college students: "I've spent four years in college. I haven't had time to pick up any skills."

And it lasts through the middle years, especially when a person is thinking of changing his or her career: "I'll have to go back to college, and get retrained, because otherwise I won't have any skills in my new field." Or: "Well, if I claim any skills, I'll start at a very entry kind of level."

All of this fright about the word "skills" is very common, and stems from a total misunderstanding of what the word means. A misunderstanding that is shared, we might add, by altogether too many employers, or human resources departments, and other so-called "vocational experts."

By understanding the word, you will automatically put yourself way ahead of most job-hunters. And, especially if you are weighing a change of career in midlife, or whenever, you can save yourself much wasted time on the adult folly called "I must go back to school." *Maybe* you need some further schooling, but very often it is possible to make a dramatic career-change without any retraining. It all depends. And you won't really *know* whether or not you need further schooling, until you have finished all the exercises in this workbook.

All right, then, if transferable skills are the heart of your vision and your destiny, let's see just exactly what transferable skills *are*.

Here are the most important truths you need to keep in mind about transferable, functional skills:

1. Your transferable (functional) skills are the most basic unit—the atoms—of whatever career you may choose.

   On the next page is a famous diagram of them, invented by the late Sidney A. Fine (reprinted by permission).

2. You should always claim the highest skills you legitimately can, on the basis of your past performance.

   As we see in the functional/transferable skills diagram on the next page, your transferable skills break down into three *families*, according to whether you use them with **Data (Information)**, **People**, or **Things**. And again, as this diagram makes clear, within each family there are *simple* skills, and there are higher, or *more complex* skills, so that these all can be diagrammed as inverted pyramids, with the simpler skills at the bottom, and the more complex ones in order above them.

   Incidentally, as a general rule—to which there are exceptions—each *higher* skill requires you to be able also to do all those skills listed below it. So of course you can claim *those*, as well. But you want to especially claim the highest skill you legitimately can, on each pyramid, based on what you have already proven you can do.

3. The higher your transferable skills, the more freedom you will have on any job.

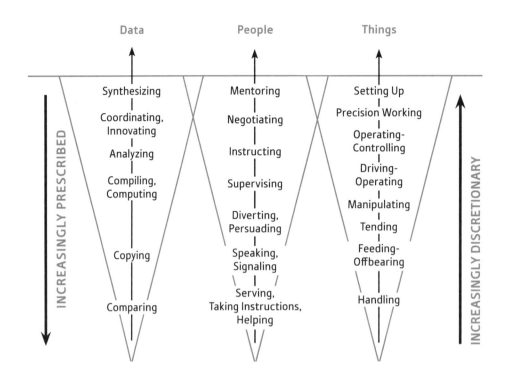

Note the side arrows and text: simpler skills can be, and usually are, heavily *prescribed* (by the employer), so if you claim *only* the simpler skills, you will have to *"fit in"*—following the instructions of your supervisor, and doing exactly what you are told to do. The *higher* the skills you can legitimately claim, the more you will be given discretion to carve out the job the way you want to—so that it truly fits *you*.

4. **The higher your transferable skills, the less competition you will face for whatever job you are seeking, because jobs that use such skills will rarely be advertised through normal channels.**

Not for you the way of classified ads, resumes, and agencies. Once you have identified your favorite transferable skills, and your favorite special knowledges, you may then approach *any organization that interests you, whether they have a known vacancy or not.* Naturally, whatever places you visit—and particularly those that have not advertised any vacancy—you will find far fewer job-hunters that you have to compete with.

In fact, if the employers you visit happen to like you well enough, they may be willing to create for you a job that does not presently exist. *In which case, you will be competing with no one, since you will be the sole applicant for that newly created job.* While this doesn't happen all the time, it is astounding to me how many times it *does* happen. *The reason* it does is that the employers often have been *thinking* about creating a new job within their organization, for quite some time—but with this and that, they just have never gotten around to *doing* it. Until you walked in.

Then they decide they don't want to let you get away, since *good employees are as hard to find as good employers.* And they suddenly remember that job they have been thinking about creating for many weeks or months, now. So they dust off their *intention*, create the job on the spot, and offer it to you! And if that new job is not only what *they* need, but is exactly what *you* were looking for, then you have a dream job. Match-match. Win-win. No, I'm not making this up. It happens, often, to those who truly know who they are.

5. **Don't confuse transferable skills with traits.**

Functional/transferable skills are often confused with **traits**, **temperaments**, or **type.** People think transferable skills are such things as: *has lots of energy, gives attention to details, gets along well with people, shows determination, works well under pressure, is sympathetic, intuitive, persistent, dynamic, dependable,* etc. As mentioned earlier, these are not functional/transferable skills, but *traits*, or the *style* with which you do your transferable skills. For example, take *"gives attention to details."* If one of your *transferable skills* is *"conducting research"* then *"gives attention to details"* describes the manner or style with which you do the transferable skill called *conducting research.* If you want to know what your traits are, popular tests such as the *Myers-Briggs Type Indicator* measure that sort of thing.[7]

If you have access to the Internet, there are clues, at least, about your traits or "type":

Working Out Your Myers-Briggs Type
www.teamtechnology.co.uk/mb-intro/mb-intro.htm
An informative article about the Myers-Briggs

The 16 Personality Types
www.personalitypage.com/high-level.html
A helpful site about Myers types

What Is Your Myers-Briggs Personality Type?
www.personalitypathways.com/type_inventory.html
www.personalitypathways.com
Another article about personality types, as well as a Myers-Briggs Applications page, with links to test resources

---

7. The Myers-Briggs Type Indicator, or "MBTI®," measures what is called *psychological type.* For further reading about this, see:

Paul D. Tieger and Barbara Barron-Tieger, *Do What You Are: Discover the Perfect Career for You Through the Secrets of Personality Type* (Revised and Updated), Fourth Edition, Little, Brown & Company, Inc., 2007. For those who cannot obtain the MBTI®, this book includes a method for readers to identify their personality types. This is one of the most popular career books in the world. It's easy to see why. Many have found great help from the concept of personality type, and the Tiegers are masters in explaining this approach to career-choice. Highly recommended.

Donna Dunning, *What's Your Type of Career? Unlock the Secrets of Your Personality to Find Your Perfect Career Path,* Nicholas Brealey Publishing, 2010. This is a dynamite book on personality type. Donna Dunning's knowledge of "Type" is encyclopedic!

David Keirsey and Marilyn Bates, *Please Understand Me: Character & Temperament Types,* B&D Books, 1984. Includes the Keirsey Temperament Sorter, or "KTS®"—again, for those who cannot obtain the MBTI® (Myers-Briggs Type Indicator).

Myers-Briggs Foundation home page
www.myersbriggs.org
The official website of the Foundation; lots of testing resources

Human Metrics Test (Jung Typology)
www.humanmetrics.com/cgi-win/JTypes2.asp
Free test, loosely based on the Myers-Briggs

Myers-Briggs Type Indicator Online
www.discoveryourpersonality.com/MBTI.html
The official Myers-Briggs test, $90

The Keirsey Temperament Sorter
http://keirsey.com
Free test, similar to the Myers-Briggs

"I Wouldn't Recognize My Skills If They Came Up and Shook Hands with Me"

Now that you know what transferable skills *are*, the problem that awaits you now, is figuring out your own. If you are one of the few lucky people who already know what your transferable skills are, blessed are you. Write them down, and put them in the order of preference, for you, on page 8 of the Flower Diagram.

If, however, you don't know what your transferable, functional skills are (and 95 percent of all workers *don't*), then you will need some help. Fortunately, we can help.

1. Write a Story (The First of Seven)

Yes, I know, I know. You can't do this exercise because you don't like to write. *Writers are a very rare breed.* That's what thousands of people have told me, over the years. And for years I kind of believed them—until blogging and texting came along. So, now we know: we human beings are "a writing people," and we only need a topic we have a real passion for, or interest in, for the writing genie to spring forth from within each of us, pen or keyboard in hand.

So, call the *Seven Stories* you're about to write your personal *offline blog*, if you prefer. But start writing. Please. Your story doesn't have to be about work. It can be about your leisure time.

Here is a specific example:

"A number of years ago, I wanted to be able to take a summer trip with my wife and four children. I had a very limited budget, and could not afford to put my family up in motels. I decided to rig our station wagon as a camper.

"First I went to the library to get some books on campers. I read those books. Next I designed a plan of what I had to build, so that I could outfit the inside of the station wagon, as well as topside.

Then I went and purchased the necessary wood. On weekends, over a period of six weeks, I first constructed, in my driveway, the shell for the 'second story' on my station wagon. Then I cut doors, windows, and placed a six-drawer bureau within that shell. I mounted it on top of the wagon, and pinioned it in place by driving two-by-fours under the station wagon's rack on top. I then outfitted the inside of the station wagon, back in the wheel-well, with a table and a bench on either side, that I made.

"The result was a complete homemade camper, which I put together when we were about to start our trip, and then disassembled after we got back home. When we went on our summer trip, we were able to be on the road for four weeks, yet stayed within our budget, since we didn't have to stay at motels. I estimate I saved $1,900 on motel bills, during that summer's vacation."

Ideally, each story you write should have the following parts, as illustrated above:

1. **Your goal: what you wanted to accomplish:** *"I wanted to be able to take a summer trip with my wife and four children."*

2. **Some kind of hurdle, obstacle, or constraint that you faced** (self-imposed or otherwise): *"I had a very limited budget, and could not afford to put my family up in motels."*

3. **A description of what you did, step by step** (how you set about to ultimately achieve your goal, above, in spite of this hurdle or constraint): *"I decided to rig our station wagon as a camper. First I went to the library to get some books on campers. I read those books. Next I designed a plan of what I had to build, so that I could outfit the inside of the station wagon, as*

well as topside. Then I went and purchased the necessary wood. On weekends, over a period of six weeks, I . . ." etc., etc.

4. **A description of the outcome or result:** *"When we went on our summer trip, we were able to be on the road for four weeks, yet stayed within our budget, since we didn't have to stay at motels."*

5. **Any measurable/quantifiable statement of that outcome, that you can think of:** *"I estimate I saved $1,900 on motel bills, during that summer's vacation."*

Now write *your* story, using the previous example as a guide.

On the following page is a form to help you write your story. Use an additional sheet of paper if you need more writing space.

Incidentally, don't necessarily try to find a story where you achieved something *big*. At least to begin with, write a story about a time when you had fun!

Do not try to be too brief. This isn't Twitter.

If you absolutely can't think of any experiences you've had where you enjoyed yourself, and accomplished something, then try this: describe the seven most enjoyable jobs that you've had; or seven roles you've had so far in your life, such as: wife, mother, cook, homemaker, volunteer in the community, citizen, dressmaker, student, etc. Tell us something you did or accomplished, in each role.

2. Analyze Your Story, to See What Transferable Skills You Used

At the top of page 38, write the title of your first story *above* the number 1. Then work your way down the column *below* that number 1, asking yourself in each case: "Did I use this transferable skill in *this story*?"

If the answer is "Yes," color the little square in under #1, with a red pen or whatever you choose.

Work your way through the entire Parachute Skills Grid that way, with just your first story. Then, voilà! You are done with Story #1. However, "one swallow doth not a summer make," so the fact that you used certain skills in this first story doesn't tell you much. What you want to find are **patterns**—transferable skills that keep reappearing in story after story of yours. They keep reappearing because they are your favorites (assuming you chose stories where you were *really* enjoying yourself).

Your Goal (what you wanted to accomplish):

Some Kind of Obstacle (or Limit, Hurdle, or Restraint) You Had to Overcome Before It Could Be Accomplished:

What You Did Step-by-Step (it may help if you pretend you are telling this story to a whining four-year-old child who keeps asking, after each of your sentences, "An' then whadja do? An' then whadja do?"):

Description of the Result (what you accomplished):

Any Measure or Quantities to Prove Your Achievement:

THE PARACHUTE SKILLS GRID

Your Seven Stories

In the space to the left, write above each number, in turn, the name you give to each story. Begin with Story #1. After you have written it, give it a name. Enter that name here (turn page on its side) above #1.

1	2	3	4	5	6	7	Skills with People; as my story shows, I can ...
							Initiate, lead, be a pioneer
							Supervise, manage
							Follow through, get things done
							Motivate
							Persuade, sell, recruit
							Consult
							Advise
							Coordinate
							Negotiate, resolve conflicts
							Help people link up or connect
							Heal, cure
							Assess, evaluate, treat
							Convey warmth and empathy
							Interview, draw out
							Raise people's self-esteem
							Instruct
							Teach, tutor, or train (individuals, groups, animals)
							Speak
							Listen
							Counsel, guide, mentor
							Communicate well, in person
							Communicate well, in writing
							Divert, amuse, entertain, perform, act
							Play an instrument
							Interpret, speak, or read a foreign language
							Serve, care for, follow instructions faithfully
1	2	3	4	5	6	7	Skills with Data, Ideas; as my story shows, I can ...
							Use my intuition
							Create, innovate, invent
							Design, use artistic abilities, be original

1	2	3	4	5	6	7	Skills with Data, Ideas; as my story shows, I can ... *(continued)*
							Visualize, including in three dimensions
							Imagine
							Use my brain
							Synthesize, combine parts into a whole
							Systematize, prioritize
							Organize, classify
							Perceive patterns
							Analyze, break down into its parts
							Work with numbers, compute
							Remember people, or data, to unusual degree
							Develop, improve
							Solve problems
							Plan
							Program
							Research
							Examine, inspect, compare, see similarities and differences
							Pay attention to details
							Use acute senses (hearing, smell, taste, sight)
							Study, observe
							Compile, keep records, file, retrieve
							Copy
1	2	3	4	5	6	7	Skills with Things, or My Favorite Medium; as my story shows, I can ...
							Control, expedite things
							Make, produce, manufacture
							Repair
							Finish, restore, preserve
							Construct
							Shape, model, sculpt
							Cut, carve, chisel
							Set up, assemble
							Handle, tend, feed
							Operate, drive
							Manipulate
							Use my body, hands, fingers, with unusual dexterity or strength

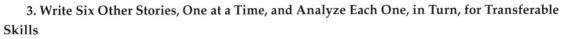

3. Write Six Other Stories, One at a Time, and Analyze Each One, in Turn, for Transferable Skills

Write Story #2 from any period in your life, analyze it using the grid, etc., etc. And keep this process up, until you have written, and analyzed, seven stories.

If you are finding it difficult to come up with seven stories, it may help you to know how others chose one or more of their stories:[8]

As I look back, I realize I chose a story that:

- Is somehow abnormal or inconsistent with the rest of my life
- Reveals my skills in a public way
- Is in a field (such as leisure, learning, etc.) far removed from my work
- I remembered through or because of its outcome
- Represented a challenge/gave me pride because it was something:
    - I previously could not do
    - My friends could not do
    - I was not supposed to be able to do
    - Only my father/mother could do, I thought
    - Only authorized/trained/experts were supposed to be able to do
    - Somebody told me I could not do
    - My peers did not do/could not do
    - The best/brilliant/famous could or could not do
    - I did not have the right degree/training to do
    - People of the opposite sex usually do
- I would like to do again:
    - In a similar/different setting
    - With similar/different people
    - For free for a change/for money for a change
- Excited me because:
    - I never did it before
    - It was forbidden
    - I took a physical risk
    - I was taking a financial risk
    - No one had ever done it before
    - It demanded a long and persistent (physical/mental) effort
    - It made me even with someone
- I loved doing because:
    - I kind of like this sort of thing
    - The people involved were extremely nice
    - It did not cost me anything
- Will support/justify the professional goals I have already chosen

---

8. Copyright © 1978, by Daniel Porot.

MY SECOND LIFE STORY

Your Goal (what you wanted to accomplish):

Some Kind of Obstacle (or Limit, Hurdle, or Restraint) You Had to Overcome Before It Could Be Accomplished:

What You Did Step-by-Step (it may help if you pretend you are telling this story to a whining four-year-old child who keeps asking, after each of your sentences, "An' then whadja do? An' then whadja do?"):

Description of the Result (what you accomplished):

Any Measure or Quantities to Prove Your Achievement:

Your Goal (what you wanted to accomplish):

Some Kind of Obstacle (or Limit, Hurdle, or Restraint) You Had to Overcome Before It Could Be Accomplished:

What You Did Step-by-Step (it may help if you pretend you are telling this story to a whining four-year-old child who keeps asking, after each of your sentences, "An' then whadja do? An' then whadja do?"):

Description of the Result (what you accomplished):

Any Measure or Quantities to Prove Your Achievement:

Your Goal (what you wanted to accomplish):

Some Kind of Obstacle (or Limit, Hurdle, or Restraint) You Had to Overcome Before It Could Be Accomplished:

What You Did Step-by-Step (it may help if you pretend you are telling this story to a whining four-year-old child who keeps asking, after each of your sentences, "An' then whadja do? An' then whadja do?"):

Description of the Result (what you accomplished):

Any Measure or Quantities to Prove Your Achievement:

Your Goal (what you wanted to accomplish):

Some Kind of Obstacle (or Limit, Hurdle, or Restraint) You Had to Overcome Before It Could Be Accomplished:

What You Did Step-by-Step (it may help if you pretend you are telling this story to a whining four-year-old child who keeps asking, after each of your sentences, "An' then whadja do? An' then whadja do?"):

Description of the Result (what you accomplished):

Any Measure or Quantities to Prove Your Achievement:

Your Goal (what you wanted to accomplish):

Some Kind of Obstacle (or Limit, Hurdle, or Restraint) You Had to Overcome Before It Could Be Accomplished:

What You Did Step-by-Step (it may help if you pretend you are telling this story to a whining four-year-old child who keeps asking, after each of your sentences, "An' then whadja do? An' then whadja do?"):

Description of the Result (what you accomplished):

Any Measure or Quantities to Prove Your Achievement:

Your Goal (what you wanted to accomplish):

Some Kind of Obstacle (or Limit, Hurdle, or Restraint) You Had to Overcome Before It Could Be Accomplished:

What You Did Step-by-Step (it may help if you pretend you are telling this story to a whining four-year-old child who keeps asking, after each of your sentences, "An' then whadja do? An' then whadja do?"):

Description of the Result (what you accomplished):

Any Measure or Quantities to Prove Your Achievement:

4. Patterns and Priorities

When you've finished this whole inventory, for all seven of your accomplishments/achievements/jobs/roles or whatever, you want to look for PATTERNS and PRIORITIES.

a. For Patterns, because it isn't a matter of whether you used a skill once only, but rather whether you used it again and again. "Once" proves nothing; "again and again" is convincing.

b. For Priorities (that is, which skills are most important to you), because the job you eventually choose may not be able to use all of your skills. You need to know *what you are willing to trade off, and what you are not.* This requires that you know which skills, or family of skills, are most important to you.

So, after finishing your seven stories (or if you're in a hurry, at least five), look through the Skills Grid on pages 38–39, now, and pick out by guess and instinct, what you think are your top ten favorite skills: not the ones you think the job-market will like the best, but the ones *you* enjoy using the most. Put those ten in Section A of the Prioritizing Grid on the next page, and prioritize them.

When you've finished with the Section D list, copy it onto the graphic below, as well as onto your Favorite Transferable Skills petal, on page 8.

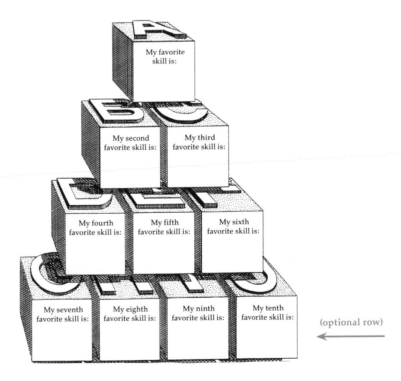

My favorite skill is:

My second favorite skill is:

My third favorite skill is:

My fourth favorite skill is:

My fifth favorite skill is:

My sixth favorite skill is:

My seventh favorite skill is:

My eighth favorite skill is:

My ninth favorite skill is:

My tenth favorite skill is:

(optional row)

OUR PRIORITIZING GRID FOR 10 ITEMS OR LESS

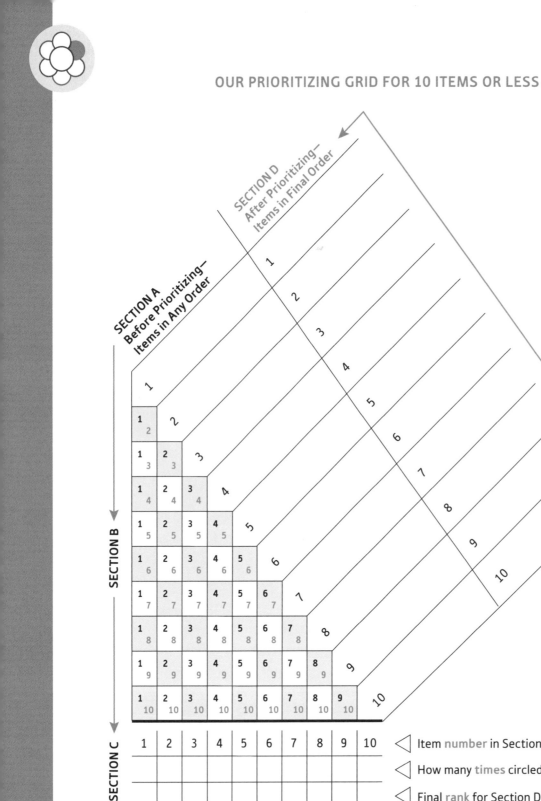

SECTION D
After Prioritizing—
Items in Final Order

SECTION A
Before Prioritizing—
Items in Any Order

SECTION B

SECTION C

Item **number** in Section A

How many **times** circled in B

Final **rank** for Section D

5. "Flesh Out" Your Favorite Transferable Skills with Your Traits

We discussed traits earlier. Traits describe:

How you deal with time, and promptness.
How you deal with people and emotions.
How you deal with authority, and being told what to do at your job.
How you deal with supervision, and being told how to do your job.
How you deal with impulse vs. self-discipline, within yourself.
How you deal with initiative vs. response, within yourself.
How you deal with crises or problems.

A Checklist of Your Strongest Traits

I am very . . .

- Accurate
- Achievement-oriented
- Adaptable
- Adept
- Adept at having fun
- Adventuresome
- Alert
- Appreciative
- Assertive
- Astute
- Authoritative
- Calm
- Cautious
- Charismatic
- Competent
- Consistent
- Contagious in my enthusiasm
- Cooperative
- Courageous
- Creative
- Decisive
- Deliberate
- Dependable/have dependability
- Diligent
- Diplomatic
- Discreet
- Driving
- Dynamic
- Effective
- Energetic
- Enthusiastic
- Exceptional
- Exhaustive
- Experienced
- Expert
- Extremely economical
- Firm
- Flexible
- Humanly oriented
- Impulsive
- Independent
- Innovative
- Knowledgeable
- Loyal
- Methodical
- Objective
- Open-minded
- Outgoing
- Outstanding
- Patient
- Penetrating
- Perceptive
- Persevering
- Persistent
- Pioneering
- Practical
- Professional
- Protective
- Punctual
- Quick/work quickly
- Rational
- Realistic
- Reliable
- Resourceful
- Responsible
- Responsive
- Safeguarding
- Self-motivated
- Self-reliant
- Sensitive
- Sophisticated, very sophisticated
- Strong
- Supportive
- Tactful
- Thorough
- Unique
- Unusual
- Versatile
- Vigorous

You need to flesh out a skill-description for six or more of your favorite skills so that you are able to describe each of your talents or skills with more than just a one-word verb or gerund, like *organizing*.

Let's take *organizing* as our example. You tell us proudly: "I'm good at organizing." That's a fine start at defining your skills, but unfortunately it doesn't yet tell us much. Organizing WHAT? People, as at a party? Nuts and bolts, as on a workbench? Or lots of information, as on a computer? These are three entirely different skills. The one word *organizing* doesn't tell us which one is yours.

So, please flesh out each of your favorite transferable skills with an object—some kind of Data/Information, or some kind of People, or some kind of Thing, and then add a Trait (adverb or adjective).

Why adjectives? Well, "I'm good at organizing information painstakingly and logically" and "I'm good at organizing information in a flash, by intuition," are two entirely different skills. The difference between them is spelled out not in the verb, nor in the object, but in the adjectival or adverbial phrase there at the end. So, expand each definition of six or more of your favorite skills, in the fashion I have just described, and add them to the Traits section of the Transferable Skills petal on page 8.

> When you want to be able to explain what makes you different from nineteen other people who can basically do the same thing that you can do, it is often the adjective or adverb that most accurately describes that difference.

Now, on to another side of Who You Are.

PETAL 4

I Am a Person Who . . .
Has Favorite Working Conditions

FOURTH PETAL:
My Favorite Working Conditions

Plants that grow beautifully at sea level, often perish if they're taken ten thousand feet up the mountain. Likewise, we do our best work under certain conditions, but not under others. Thus, the question, "What are your favorite working conditions?" actually is a question about "Under what circumstances do you do your most effective work?"

As I just mentioned, the best way to approach this is by starting with the things you *disliked* about all your previous jobs, using the chart on the next page to list these. Copy this chart onto a piece of notebook paper if you wish, before you begin filling it out. *Column A may begin with such factors as: "too noisy," "too much supervision," "no windows in my workplace," "having to be at work by 6 a.m.," etc.*

If you are baffled as to how to prioritize the Column A list in the space provided for that ranking (Column B), I recommend you use the Prioritizing Grid on page 54. (For a refresher on how to use it, turn to "Instructions for Using the Prioritizing Grid," page 22.) This time, when you compare each pair of items, the question you must ask yourself is, "If I were offered two jobs, and in the first job offer I would be rid of my first distasteful working condition but not the second, while in the second job offer I would be rid of my second distasteful working condition, but not the first, which job offer would I take?"

DISTASTEFUL WORKING CONDITIONS

	Column A — **Distasteful Working Conditions**
Places I Have Worked Thus Far in My Life	I Have Learned from the Past That My Effectiveness at Work Is Decreased When I Have to Work Under These Conditions

DISTASTEFUL WORKING CONDITIONS

Column B — Distasteful Working Conditions Ranked	Column C ✚ The Keys to My Effectiveness at Work
Among the Factors or Qualities Listed in Column A, These Are the Ones I Dislike Absolutely the Most (in Order of Decreasing Dislike)	I Believe My Effectiveness Would Be at an Absolute Maximum, If I Could Work Under These Conditions (The Opposite of These Qualities, in Order):
1a.	1b.
2a.	2b.
3a.	3b.
4a.	4b.
5a.	5b.
6a.	6b.
7a.	7b.
8a.	8b.
9a.	9b.
10a.	10b.

OUR PRIORITIZING GRID FOR 10 ITEMS OR LESS

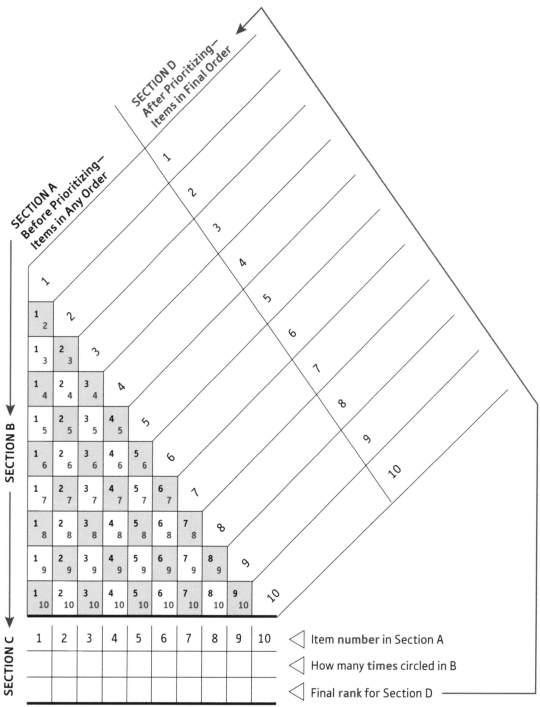

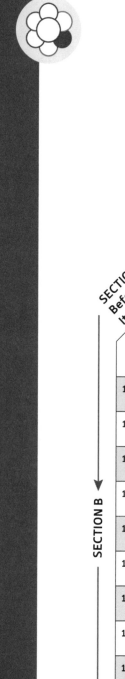

SECTION D
After Prioritizing—
Items in Final Order

SECTION A
Before Prioritizing—
Items in Any Order

SECTION B

SECTION C

◁ Item **number** in Section A

◁ How many **times** circled in B

◁ Final **rank** for Section D

After you've finished prioritizing, what have you ended up with, in Section D? The exact list you copy into Column B of your Distasteful Working Conditions chart, page 53.

Now that you have that list in Column B, ranked in terms of most distasteful down to least distasteful working conditions, turn to Column C in that chart and write the *opposite*, or something near the *opposite*, directly across from each item in Column B.

Copy the top five items in Column C onto the Favorite Working Conditions petal of your Flower Diagram, page 9.

Now, on to another side of Who You Are.

PETAL 5

I Am a Person Who . . .
Prefers a Certain Level of Income and Responsibility

FIFTH PETAL:
My Preferred Salary and Level of Responsibility

Money is important. Or else we've got to barter for our food, clothing, and shelter. So, when we're out of work, unless we have huge amounts of money in our savings account or investments, we are inevitably thinking: "What am I going to do, so that I have enough money to put food on the table, clothes on our backs, and a roof over our heads for myself—and for my family or partner *(if I have one)?*"

Happiness is important, too. So, we may find ourselves thinking: "How much do I really need to be earning, for me to be truly happy with my life?"

Are these two worries—money and happiness—related? Can money buy happiness?

Partly, it turns out. Partly. A study, published in 2010, of the responses of 450,000 people in the U.S. to a daily survey, found that the less money they made, the more unhappy they tended to be, day after day.[9] No surprise, there. And, obviously, the more money they made, measured in terms of percentage improvement, the happier they tended to be, *as measured by the frequency and intensity of moments of smiling, laughter, affection, and joy all day long, vs. moments of sadness, worry, and stress.*

So, money does buy happiness. But only up to a point. That point was found to be around $75,000 annual income (*at the end of 2011, median household income was $51,413*[10]). If people

9. Research by Daniel Kahneman and Angus Deaton, published in the *Proceedings of the National Academy of Sciences*, Early Edition, September 6, 2010.
10. According to Sentier Research, reported by Paul Davidson, "U.S. Median Household Income Up 4% at End of 2011," *USA Today*, February 9, 2012.

made more than $75,000, it of course further improved their *satisfaction* with how their life was going, but it did not increase their *happiness*. Above $75,000, they started to report reduced ability to spend time with people they liked, to enjoy leisure, and to savor small pleasures. Happiness depends on things like that, and on other factors too: good health, a loving relationship, loving friends, a feeling of competence, gaining mastery, respect, praise, or even love, because we are really good at what we do.

So, this petal cannot be filled out all by itself. It is inextricably tied to the other petals—most particularly, to what you love to do, and where you love to do it.

Still, salary is something you must think out ahead of time, when you're contemplating your ideal job or career. Level goes hand in hand with salary, of course.

1. The first question here is at what level would you like to work, in your ideal job?

Level is a matter of how much responsibility you want, in an organization:

❑ Boss or CEO (this may mean you'll have to form your own business)
❑ Manager or someone under the boss who carries out orders
❑ The head of a team
❑ A member of a team of equals
❑ One who works in tandem with one other partner
❑ One who works alone, either as an employee or as a consultant to an organization, or as a one-person business

Enter a two- or three-word summary of your answer on the Preferred Salary and Level of Responsibility petal of your Flower Diagram, page 9.

2. The second question here is what salary would you like to be aiming for?

Here you have to think in terms of minimum or maximum. **Minimum** is what you would need to make, if you were just barely "getting by." And you need to know this *before* you go in for a job interview with anyone (*or before you form your own business, and need to know how much profit you must make, just to survive*).

Maximum could be any astronomical figure you can think of, but what is more useful here is a salary you realistically think you could make, with your present competency and experience, were you working for a real, *but generous*, boss. (If this maximum figure is still depressingly low, then think of the salary you would like to be making five years from now.)

Prepare two different versions of the following budget: **one** with the amount you'd ideally *like* to make, and **the other** a minimum budget, which will give you the floor below which you simply cannot afford to go.

Make out a detailed outline of your estimated expenses *now*, listing what you need (minimum) and want (maximum) *monthly* in the following categories:[11]

MIN ⟵——⟶ MAX

	MIN	MAX
Housing		
Rent or mortgage payments	$	$
Electricity/gas	$	$
Water	$	$
Phone/Internet	$	$
Garbage removal	$	$
Cleaning, maintenance, repairs[12]	$	$
Food		
What you spend at the supermarket and/or farmer's market, etc.	$	$
Eating out	$	$
Clothing		
Purchase of new or used clothing	$	$
Cleaning, dry cleaning, laundry	$	$
Automobile/transportation		
Car payments	$	$
Gas (who knows?)[13]	$	$
Repairs	$	$
Public transportation (*bus, train, plane*)	$	$

11. If this kind of financial figuring is not your cup of tea, find a buddy, friend, relative, family member, or anyone, who can help you do this. If you don't know anyone who could do this, go to your local church, synagogue, religious center, social club, gym, or wherever you hang out, and ask the leader or manager there, to help you find someone. If there's a bulletin board, put up a notice on the bulletin board.
12. If you have extra household expenses, such as a security system, be sure to include the quarterly (or whatever) expenses here, divided by three, in order to arrive at a monthly figure.
13. Your checkbook stubs and/or online banking records will tell you a lot of this stuff. But you may be vague about your cash or credit card expenditures. For example, you may not know how much you spend at the supermarket, or how much you spend on gas, etc. But there is a simple way to find out. Keep notes on your Smartphone or iPad for two weeks (there are apps for that), jotting down everything you pay cash (or use credit cards) for—on the spot, right after you pay it. At the end of those two weeks, you'll be able to take that notepad and make a realistic guess of what should be put down in these categories that now puzzle you. (Multiply the two-week figure by two, and you'll have the monthly figure.)

Insurance	MIN	MAX
Car	$	$
Medical or health care	$	$
House and personal possessions	$	$
Life	$	$
Medical expenses		
Doctors' visits	$	$
Prescriptions	$	$
Fitness costs	$	$
Support for other family members		
Child-care costs (*if you have children*)	$	$
Child-support (*if you're paying that*)	$	$
Support for your parents (*if you're helping out*)	$	$
Charity giving/tithe (*to help others*)	$	$
School/learning		
Children's costs (*if you have children in school*)	$	$
Your learning costs (*adult education, job-hunting classes, etc.*)	$	$
Pet care (*if you have pets*)	$	$
Bills and debts (*usual monthly payments*)		
Credit cards	$	$
Local stores	$	$
Other obligations you pay off monthly	$	$
Taxes		
Federal[14] (*next April's taxes due, divided by months remaining until then*)	$	$
State (*likewise*)	$	$
Local/property (*next amount due, divided by months remaining until then*)	$	$
Tax-help (*if you ever use an accountant, pay a friend to help you with taxes, etc.*)	$	$
Savings	$	$
Retirement (Keogh, IRA, SEP, etc.)	$	$
Amusement/discretionary spending		
Movies, television, video rentals, etc.	$	$
Other kinds of entertainment	$	$
Reading, newspapers, magazines, books	$	$
Gifts (birthday, Christmas, etc.)	$	$
Vacations	$	$
Total Amount You Need Each Month	$	$

14. Incidentally, for U.S. citizens, looking ahead to next April 15, be sure to check with your local IRS office or a reputable accountant to find out if you can deduct the expenses of your job-hunt on your federal (and state) income tax returns. At this writing, some job-hunters can, if—big IF—this is not your first job that you're looking for, if you haven't been unemployed too long, and if you aren't making a career-change. Do go find out what the latest "ifs" are. If the IRS says you are eligible, keep careful receipts of everything related to your job-hunt, as you go along: telephone calls, stationery, printing, postage, travel, etc.

Multiply the total amount you need each month by 12, to get the yearly figure. Divide the yearly figure by 2,000, and you will be reasonably near the hourly wage. Thus, if you need $3,333 per month, multiplied by 12, that's $40,000 a year, and then divided by 2,000, that's $20 an hour.

Now, enter the salary range and any notes you want to add, about the level of responsibility you want to take on, to justify this salary, plus any "non-monetary" rewards you seek, on the Preferred Salary and Level of Responsibility petal, found on page 9.

Optional Exercise

You may wish to put down other rewards, besides money, that you would hope for, from your next job or career. These might be:

- ❏ Adventure
- ❏ Challenge
- ❏ Respect
- ❏ Influence
- ❏ Popularity
- ❏ Fame
- ❏ Power
- ❏ Intellectual stimulation from the other workers there

- ❏ A chance to be creative
- ❏ A chance to help others
- ❏ A chance to exercise leadership
- ❏ A chance to make decisions
- ❏ A chance to use your expertise
- ❏ A chance to bring others closer to God
- ❏ Other:

If you do check off things on this list, arrange your answers in order of importance to you, and then add them to the petal.

Now, we turn to another side of Who You Are.

PETAL 6

I Am a Person Who . . .
Prefers Certain Places to Live

SIXTH PETAL:
My Preferred Place(s) to Live

If you are doing this exercise with a partner, make a copy of the following chart for them, so that each of you is working on a clean copy of your own, and can follow these instructions independently. It can be a photocopy or a handwritten copy on a larger (11" x 17") piece of paper or cardboard, which you can obtain from any arts and crafts store or "stationery" section of your local supermarket.

1. In *Column 1*, each of you should list all the places where you have ever lived.

2. In *Column 2*, each of you should list all the factors you disliked (and still dislike) about each place. The factors do not have to be put exactly opposite the name in *Column 1*. The names in *Column 1* exist simply to jog your memory.

   If, as you go, you remember some good things about any place, put those factors at the bottom of the next column, *Column 3*.

   If the same factors keep repeating, just put a checkmark after the first listing of that factor, every time it repeats.

   Keep going until you have listed all the factors you disliked or hated about each and every place you named in *Column 1*. Now, in effect, throw away *Column 1*; discard it from your thoughts. The negative factors were what you were after. *Column 1* has served its purpose.

3. Look at *Column 2*, now, your list of negative factors, and in *Column 3* try to list each one's opposite (or near opposite). For example, "the sun never shone, there" would, in *Column 3*, be turned into "mostly sunny, all year 'round." It will not always be *the exact opposite*. For example, the negative factor "rains all the time" does not necessarily translate into the positive "sunny all the time." It might be something like "sunny at least 200 days a year." It's your call. Keep going, until every negative factor in *Column 2* is turned into its opposite, a positive factor, in *Column 3*. At the bottom, note the positive factors you already listed there, when you were working on *Column 2*.

4. In *Column 4*, now, list the positive factors in *Column 3*, in the order of most important (to you), down to least important (to you). For example, if you were looking at, and trying to name a new town, city, or place where you could be happy and flourish, what is the first thing you would look for? Would it be, good weather? or lack of crime? or good schools? or access to cultural opportunities, such as music, art, museums, or whatever? or would it be inexpensive housing? etc., etc. Rank all the factors in *Column 4*. Use the Prioritzing Grid on page 66 if you need to.

5. If you are doing this by yourself, list on a *worksheet* or "scribble sheet" the top ten factors, in order of importance to you, and show it to everyone you meet for the next ten days, with the ultimate question: "Can you think of places that have these ten factors,

(continued on page 67)

My Geographical Preferences **DECISION MAKING FOR JUST YOU**		
Column 1	**Column 2**	**Column 3**
Names of Places I Have Lived	**From the Past: Negatives**	**Translating the Negatives into Positives**
		Factors I Liked and Still Like About Any Place

My Geographical Preferences DECISION MAKING FOR JUST YOU	
Column 4	Column 5
Ranking of My Positives	Places That Fit These Criteria
1.	
2.	
3.	
4.	
5.	
6.	
7.	
8.	
9.	
10.	

Our Geographical Preferences DECISION MAKING FOR YOU AND A PARTNER		
Column 6	Column 7	Column 8
Ranking of His/Her Preferences	Combining Our Two Lists (Columns 4 and 6)	Places That Fit These Criteria
a.	a.	
	1.	
b.	b.	
	2.	
c.	c.	
	3.	
d.	d.	
	4.	
e.	e.	
	5.	
f.	f.	
	6.	
g.	g.	
	7.	
h.	h.	
	8.	
i.	i.	
	9.	
j.	j.	
	10.	

OUR PRIORITIZING GRID FOR 10 ITEMS OR LESS

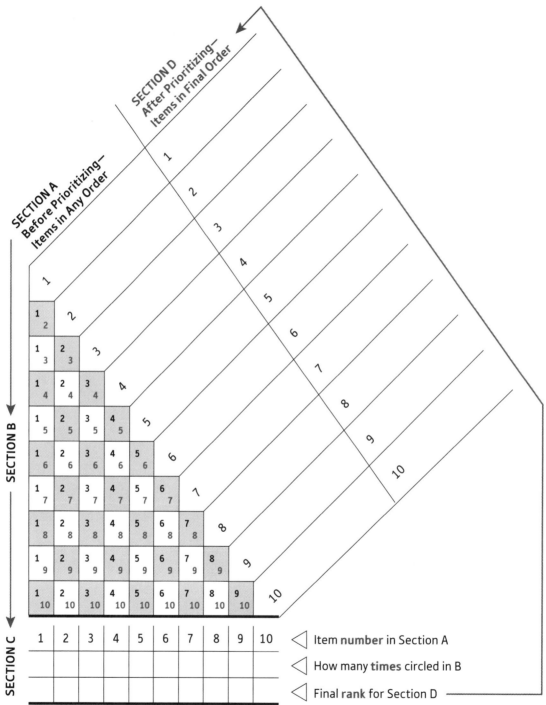

SECTION D
After Prioritizing—
Items in Final Order

SECTION A
Before Prioritizing—
Items in Any Order

SECTION B

SECTION C

	1	2	3	4	5	6	7	8	9	10

◁ Item **number** in Section A

◁ How many **times** circled in B

◁ Final **rank** for Section D

or at least the top five?" Jot down their suggestions on the back of the *scribble sheet*. When the ten days are up, look at the back of your sheet and circle the three places that seem the most interesting to you. If there is only a partial overlap between your dream factors and the places your friends and acquaintances suggested, *make sure the overlap is in the factors that count the most*. Now you have some names that you will want to find out more about, until you are sure which is your absolute favorite place to live, and then your second, and third, as backups.

Put the names of the three places, and/or your top five geographical factors, on the Flower Diagram, on the Preferred Places to Live petal, page 9.

6. If you are doing this with a partner, skip *Column 5*. Instead, when you have finished your *Column 4*, look at your partner's *Column 4*, and copy it into *Column 6*. The numbering of *your* list in *Column 4* is 1, 2, 3, 4, etc. Your partner's list, as you copy it into *Column 6*, is a, b, c, d, etc.

7. Now, in *Column 7*, combine your *Column 4* with *Column 6* (your partner's preferences, renumbered). Both of you can work now from just one person's chart. Combine the two lists as illustrated on the chart: first your partner's top favorite geographical factor ("a"), then *your* top favorite geographical factor ("1"), then your partner's second most important favorite geographical factor ("b"), then yours ("2"), etc., until you have twenty favorite geographical factors (*yours and your partner's*) listed, in order, in *Column 7*.

8. List on a *scribble sheet* the top ten factors, and both of you should show it to everyone you meet, for the next ten days, with the same question as above: "Can you think of any places that have these ten factors, or at least the top five?" Jot down their suggestions on the back of the *scribble sheet*. When the ten days are up, you and your partner should look at the back of your sheet and circle the three places that look the most interesting to the two of you. If there is only a partial overlap between your dream factors and the places your friends and acquaintances suggested, make sure the overlap is in the factors that matter the most to the two of you, i.e., the ones that are at the top of your list in *Column 7*. Now you have some names of places that you will want to find out more about, until you are sure which is the absolute favorite place to live for both of you, and then your second, and third, as backups.

Put the names of the top three places, and/or your top five geographical factors, on the Flower Diagram, on the Preferred Places to Live petal, page 9.

And now we turn to the last side of Who You Are.

I Am a Person Who . . .
Has a Certain Goal, Purpose, or Mission in Life

SEVENTH PETAL:
My Goal, Purpose, or Mission in Life

As John L. Holland famously said, "We need to look further down the road than just headlight range at night." The road is the road of Life. You need to dream about the broad outcome of your life, and not just this present time in your life. What kind of footprint do you want to leave on this earth, after your journey here is done? Figure that out, and you're well on your way to defining your life as having purpose and mission.

The Nine Kingdoms of Mission and Purpose

Generally speaking, mission breaks down into nine kingdoms—corresponding to our human nature. As you look these over, the question is, which one appeals to *you* the most? Time for some hard thinking (ouch!). So, read on, *slowly.* Take time to ponder and think.

1. **The Mind.** The question is: *When you have finished your life here on earth, do you want there to be more knowledge, truth, or clarity in the world, because you were here? Knowledge, truth, or clarity concerning* what *in particular?* If this describes You, then your need for purpose is pointing you toward the kingdom of the mind.

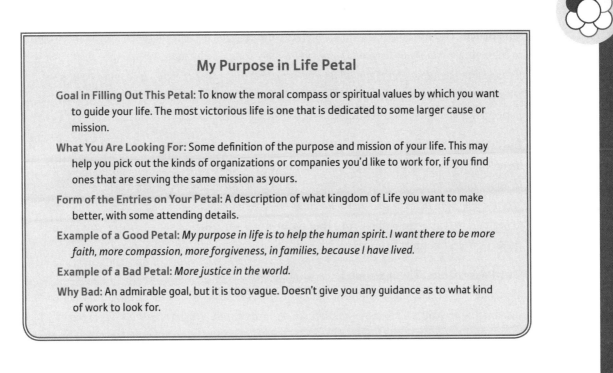

2. **The Body.** The question is: *When you have finished your life here on earth, do you want there to be more wholeness, fitness, or health in the world, more binding up of the body's wounds and strength, more feeding of the hungry, and clothing of the poor, because you were here? What issue in particular?* If this describes You, then your need for purpose is pointing you toward the kingdom of the body.

3. **The Eyes and Other Senses.** The question is: *When you have finished your life here on earth, do you want there to be more beauty in the world, because you were here? If so, what kind of beauty entrances you? Is it art, music, flowers, photography, painting, staging, crafts, clothing, jewelry, or what?* If this describes You, then your need for purpose is pointing you toward the kingdom of the eyes and senses.

4. **The Heart.** The question is: *When you have finished your life here on earth, do you want there to be more love and compassion in the world, because you were here? Love or compassion for whom? Or for what?* If this describes You, then your need for purpose is pointing you toward the kingdom of the heart.

5. **The Will or Conscience.** The question is: *When you have finished your life here on earth, do you want there to be more morality, more justice, more righteousness, more honesty in the world, because you were here? In what areas of human life or history, in particular? And in what geographical area?* If this describes You, then your need for purpose is pointing you toward the kingdom of the conscience.

6. **The Spirit.** The question is: *When you have finished your life here on earth, do you want there to be more spirituality in the world, more faith, more compassion, more forgiveness, more love for God and the human family in all its diversity, because you were here? If so, with what ages, people, or with what parts of human life?* If this describes You, then your need for purpose is pointing you toward the kingdom of the spirit, or (if you prefer) *The Kingdom of God.*

7. **Entertainment.** The question is: *When you have finished your life here on earth, do you want there to be more lightening of people's loads, more giving them perspective, more helping them to forget their cares for a spell; do you want there to be more laughter in the world, and joy, because you were here? If so, what particular kind of entertainment do you want to contribute to the world?* If this describes You, then your need for purpose is pointing you toward the kingdom of entertainment.

8. **Our Possessions.** The question is: *Is your major concern the often false love of possessions in this world? When you have finished your life here on earth, do you want there to be better stewardship of what we possess—as individuals, as a community, as a nation—in the world, because you were here? Do you want to see simplicity, savings, and a broader emphasis on the word "enough," rather than on the word "more, more"? If so, in what areas of human life in particular?* If this describes You, then your need for purpose is pointing you toward the kingdom of possessions.

9. **The Earth.** The question is: *Is the planet on which we stand, your major concern? When you have finished your life here on earth, do you want there to be better protection of this fragile planet, more exploration of the world or the universe—exploration, not exploitation—more dealing with its problems and its energy, because you were here? If so, which problems or challenges in particular, draw your heart and soul?* If this describes You, then your need for purpose is pointing you toward the kingdom of the earth.

In sum, remember that all of these are worthwhile purposes and missions, all of these are necessary and needed, in this world. The question is, which one in particular draws you to it, *the most*? Which one do you most want to lend your brain, your energies, your skills and gifts, your life, to serve, while you are here on this earth?[15]

When you are done, enter a summary paragraph of what you have decided your purpose or mission is, on the Goal, Purpose, or Mission in Life petal, on page 8.

P.S. There are two challenges you may want to anticipate, in doing this particular exercise. First Challenge: You just come up empty on this exercise, despite hard thinking. No harm done. If you want an answer, just keep the question on the back-burner of your mind; eventually some insight is going to break through. Tomorrow, next week, next month, or a year from now. Relax. Be patient with yourself.

---

15. And by the way, if you want to have fun, if you have a computer go to the Internet, choose a browser like Google or Bing, and type your kingdom (*the Mind*, etc.) into the search line, and see if anything pops up that intrigues you.

Second Challenge: This petal doesn't grab you at all. Okay. Then instead of writing a statement of purpose or mission for your life, write instead a statement outlining what you think about *life*: why are we here, why are *You* here, and so on. This is often called "Your Philosophy of Life":

In writing a philosophy of life, it should be no more than two pages, single spaced, and can be less; it should address whichever of these elements you think are most important; pick and choose. You do not have to write about all of them. In most cases, you will only need two or three sentences about each element you choose to comment on.

Beauty: what kind of beauty stirs us, what the function of beauty is in the world

Behavior: how we should behave in this world

Beliefs: what our strongest beliefs are

Celebration: how we like to play or celebrate, in life

Choice: what its nature and importance is

Community: what our concept is about belonging to each other; what we think our responsibility is to each other

Compassion: what we think about its importance and use

Confusion: how we live with it, and deal with it

Death: what we think about it and what we think happens after it

Events: what we think makes things happen, how we explain why they happen

Free will: whether we are "predetermined" or have free will

God: see Supreme Being

Happiness: what makes for the truest human happiness

Heroes and heroines: who ours are, and why

Human: what we think is important about being human, what we think is our function

Love: what we think about its nature and importance, along with all its related words: compassion, forgiveness, grace

Moral issues: which ones we believe are the most important for us to pay attention to, wrestle with, help solve

Paradox: what our attitude is toward its presence in life

Purpose: why we are here, what life is all about

Reality: what we think is its nature, and components

Self: deciding whether physical self is the limit of your being, deciding what trust in self means

Spirituality: what its place is in human life, how we should treat it

Stewardship: what we should do with God's gifts to us

Supreme Being: our concept of, and what we think holds the universe together

Truth: what we think about it, which truths are most important

Uniqueness: what we think makes each of us unique

Values: what we think about ourselves, what we think about the world, prioritized as to what matters most (to us)

When you are done writing, put a summary paragraph on your Goal, Purpose, or Mission in Life petal, on page 8.

Example
(Rich Feller's Flower)

Favorite People-Environment

1. Strong social, perceptual skills
2. Emotionally and physically healthy
3. Enthusiastically include others
4. Heterogeneous in interests and skills
5. Social changers, innovators
6. Politically, economically astute
7. Confident enough to confront/cry and be foolish
8. Sensitive to nontraditional issues
9. I and R (see page 27)
10. Nonmaterialistic

Favorite Values

1. Improve the human condition
2. Promote interdependence and futuristic principles
3. Maximize productive use of human/material resources
4. Teach people to be self-directed/self-responsible
5. Free people from self-defeating controls (thoughts, rules, barriers)
6. Promote capitalistic principles
7. Reduce exploitation
8. Promote political participation
9. Acknowledge those who give to the community
10. Give away ideas

Favorite Interests

1. Large conference planning
2. Regional geography & culture
3. Traveling on $20/day
4. Career planning seminars
5. Counseling techniques/theories
6. American policies
7. Fundamentals of sports
8. Fighting sexism
9. NASCAR auto racing
10. Interior design

Favorite Skills

1. Observational/learning skills • continually expose self to new experiences • perceptive in identifying and assessing potential of others
2. Leadership skills • continually searches for more resonsibility • sees a problem/acts to solve it
3. Instructing/interpreting/guiding • committed to learning as a lifelong process • create atmosphere of acceptance
4. Serving/helping/human relations skills • shapes atmosphere of particular place • relates well in dealing with public
5. Detail/follow-through skills • handle great variety of tasks • resource broker
6. Influencing/persuading skills • recruiting talent/leadership • inspiring trust
7. Performing skills • getting up in front of a group (if I'm in control) • addressing small and large groups
8. Intuitional/innovative skills • continually develop/generate new ideas
9. Develop/plan/organize/execute • designing projects • utilizing skills of others
10. Language/read/write • communicate effectively • can think quickly on my feet

Favorite Working Conditions

1. Receive clinical supervision
2. Mentor relationship
3. Excellent secretary
4. Part of larger, highly respected organization with clear direction
5. Near gourmet and health food specialty shops
6. Heterogeneous colleagues (race, sex, age)
7. Flexible dress code
8. Merit system
9. Can bike/bus/walk to work
10. Private office with window

Geography

1. Close to major city
2. Mild winters/low humidity
3. Change in seasons
4. Clean and green
5. 100,000 people
6. Nice shopping malls
7. Wide range of athletic options
8. Diverse economic base
9. Ample local culture
10. Sense of community (pride)

Salary and Level of Responsibility

1. Can determine 9/12 month contract
2. Can determine own projects
3. Considerable clout in organization's direction without administrative responsibilities
4. Able to select colleagues
5. 3 to 5 assistants
6. $35K to $50K
7. Serve on various important boards
8. Can defer clerical and budget decisions and tasks
9. Speak before large groups
10. Can run for elected office

Readers have asked to see an example of "That One Piece of Paper" all filled out. Rich W. Feller—a student of mine back in 1982, now a world-famous professor and expert in the national career development field—filled out his flower as you see, on the preceding page. He said "That One Piece of Paper" has been his lifelong companion ever since, and his guiding star. (The petals then were slightly different.)

Rich Feller, a University Distinguished Teaching Scholar and Professor at Colorado State University, whose own personal "Flower Diagram" is on the previous page, first put his personal "picture" together almost thirty years ago. Here are his comments about its usefulness since, and how "That One Piece of Paper" helped him, how he's used it, and how it's changed.

What the Parachute Flower Has Meant to Me

More than anything I've gained from an academic life, my Flower has given me hope, direction, and a lens to satisfaction. Using it to assess my life direction during crisis, career moves, and stretch assignments, it helps me define and hold to personal commitments. In many ways it's my "guiding light." Data within my Flower became and remain the core of any success and satisfaction I have achieved.

After I first filled out my own Flower Diagram in a two-week workshop with Dick Bolles back in 1982, I decided to teach the Flower to others. My academic position has allowed me to do this, abundantly. Having now taught the Flower to thousands of counselors, career development, and human resource specialists, I continually use it with clients, and in my own transitional retirement planning.

I'm overwhelmed with how little has changed within my Flower, over the years. My Flower is the best of what I am. Its petals are my compass, and using my "favorite skills" are the mirror to a joyful day. I trust the wisdom within "That One Piece of Paper." It has guided my work and my life, ever since 1982, and it has helped my wife and I define our hopes for our son.

The process of filling out and acting on "That One Piece of Paper" taught me a lot. Specifically, it taught me **the importance of the following ten things, often running contrary to what my studies and doctoral work had taught me previously.**

I learned from my Flower the importance of:

1. Chasing after passions, honoring strengths, and respecting skill identification

2. Challenging societal definitions of balance and success

3. Committing to something bigger than oneself

4. Living authentically and with joy

5. Being good at what matters to oneself and its relationship to opportunity

6. Finding pleasure in all that one does

7. Staying focused on well-being and life satisfaction

8. Personal clarity and responsibility for designing "possible selves"

(continued)

9. Letting the world know, humbly but clearly, what we want

10. "Coaching" people amidst a world of abundance where individuals yearn for individual meaning and purpose more than they hunger for possessions, abject compliance with society's expectations, or simply fitting in

This technologically enhanced, global workplace we now face in the twenty-first century certainly challenges all we thought we knew about our life roles. Maintaining clarity, learning agility, and identifying development plans have become elevated to new and critical importance, if we are to maintain choice. As a result I've added the following four emphases to "Rich's Flower": *Have, do, learn,* and *give*. That is to say, I try to keep a running list (constantly updated) of ten things that I want to:

1. Have

2. Do

3. Learn

4. Give

Through the practice of answering the four questions listed above, I can measure change in my growth and development.

I feel so fortunate to have the opportunity to share with others how much I gained from the wisdom and hope embedded within "Rich's Flower."

I humbly offer my resume, home location and design, and family commitments on my website at **www.mycahs.colostate.edu/Rich.Feller**. I'd be honored to share my journey, and encourage others to nurture and shine light on their garden as well. I believe you'll find about 90 percent of the Flower's items influence our daily experience.

Rich Feller
Professor of Counseling and Career Development
University Distinguished Teaching Scholar
Colorado State University
Fort Collins, CO

Okay, you've got your completed Flower. A picture of who you are, in all your glory. Also, a picture of a dream job that you can now go looking for.

Egotism Versus Self-Esteem

Good self-esteem is an art. An art of *balance*. A balance between thinking too little of ourselves, and thinking too much of ourselves.

The name for thinking too much of ourselves is *egotism*. We have all run into that, at some point in our lives, so we know what it looks like. Some of us have even caught a passing glimpse of it in the mirror.

In our culture and others, we are taught to recoil from this in horror. We even have mythologies warning us against it; the ancient Greek myth of Narcissus, for example. So, in order to avoid egotism, a lot of us go way overboard in the other direction. We shrink from ever declaring that we have any virtue, any excellency, any special gifts, lest we be accused of boasting. And so we fall into that opposite pit from egotism, namely, *ingratitude*. We appear ungrateful for the gifts that life, the universe, God—you name it—has already given us.

Okay then, how do we adopt the proper attitude toward our gifts—thinking and speaking of them honestly, humbly, gratefully—without sounding egotistical? Here's the key: *the more you see your own gifts clearly, the more you must pay attention to the gifts that others have.* The more sensitive you become to how unusual you are, the more you must become sensitive to how unusual those around you are. The more you pay attention to yourself, the more you must pay attention to others. The more you ponder the mystery of You, the more you must ponder the mystery of all those you encounter, every loved one, every friend, every acquaintance, every stranger.

As I said, good self-esteem is the art of balance. A balance between thinking too little of ourselves, and thinking too much of ourselves. But we can only think too much of ourselves if we lose awareness of others.

So, look at yourself, but equally look at them—with wonder. You make yourself not stand out above others, not by diminishing yourself, but by elevating them. It is no sin to heighten your awareness of your own gifts, as long as that heightens also your awareness of the gifts that those around you have. The world is filled with talented people, you among them; but not just you.

Done!

You will now have one of two reactions as you look over your Flower.

A Lightbulb Goes On

For some of you there will be a big *Aha!* as you look at your Flower Diagram. A lightbulb will go on, over your head, and you will say, "My goodness, I see *exactly* what sort of career this points me to." This happens particularly with intuitive people.

If you are one of those intuitive people, I say, "Good for you!" Just two gentle warnings, if I may: Don't prematurely close out *other* possibilities.

And *don't* say to yourself: "Well, I see what it is that I would die to be able to do, but I *know* there is no job in the world like that, that *I* would be able to get." Dear friend, you don't know any such thing. You haven't done your research yet. Of course, it is always possible that when you've completed all that research, and conducted your search, you still may not be able to find *all* that you want—down to the last detail. But you'd be surprised at how much of your dream you may be able to find.

Other Possibility, You Look at Your Flower Diagram and . . . a Lightbulb *Doesn't* Go On

In contrast to what I just said, many of you will look at your completed Flower Diagram, and you won't have *a clue* as to what job or career it points to. Soooo, we need a "fallback" strategy.

First, write down on one piece of paper your top five skills and your top four special knowledges from your Flower, and then ask at least five friends, family members, and professionals you know what job-titles and job-fields come to mind. Then, approach contacts in that field for Informational Interviews. During Informational Interviewing, you want to talk to people who are actually doing the work you think you'd love to do. Why? In effect, you are mentally *trying on jobs* to see if they fit you.

Once you discover places you'd like to work for, do some preliminary research on them before you approach them for an interview.

And remember, always send a thank-you note to anyone who helps you along the way.

Need More Help?

This should get you started toward finding your dream job, with the Flower as your guide. For more information on job-hunting, I invite you to consult with the book for which this workbook is a companion: *What Color Is Your Parachute? A Practical Manual for Job-Hunters and Career-Changers,* by yours truly.

Don't just drop your Flower at this point. Be persistent, be thorough, and don't give up just because your Flower doesn't immediately point you toward the next step. Keep showing your Flower to anyone and everyone, and ask what suggestions they can make. This is your life you're working on, your *Life*. Make it glorious.

About the Author

RICHARD N. BOLLES (often known by his familiar name, Dick Bolles) is widely acknowledged as the founder of the modern career development field, due to his writings for the past forty years. A member of Mensa and the Society for Human Resource Management, he has been the keynote speaker at hundreds of conferences. Bolles was trained in chemical engineering at Massachusetts Institute of Technology, and holds a bachelor's degree cum laude in physics from Harvard University, a master's in sacred theology from General Theological (Episcopal) Seminary in New York City, and three honorary doctorates. He lives in the San Francisco Bay Area with his wife, Marci.

Also by Richard N. Bolles

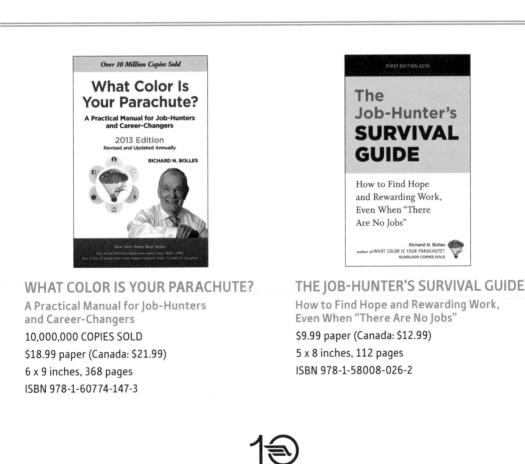

WHAT COLOR IS YOUR PARACHUTE?
A Practical Manual for Job-Hunters and Career-Changers
10,000,000 COPIES SOLD
$18.99 paper (Canada: $21.99)
6 x 9 inches, 368 pages
ISBN 978-1-60774-147-3

THE JOB-HUNTER'S SURVIVAL GUIDE
How to Find Hope and Rewarding Work, Even When "There Are No Jobs"
$9.99 paper (Canada: $12.99)
5 x 8 inches, 112 pages
ISBN 978-1-58008-026-2

Available from Ten Speed Press wherever books are sold.
www.tenspeed.com

Published in the United States by Ten Speed Press, an imprint of the Crown Publishing Group,
a division of Random House, Inc., New York.
www.crownpublishing.com
www.tenspeed.com

Ten Speed Press and the Ten Speed Press colophon are registered trademarks of Random House, Inc.

Previous editions of this work were published in 1998, 2005, and 2010 by Ten Speed Press, Berkeley, CA;
text has been adapted from chapter 5 of *What Color Is Your Parachute? 2013*.

Library of Congress Cataloging-in-Publication Data

Bolles, Richard Nelson.
  What color is your parachute? job-hunter's workbook / Richard N. Bolles. — 4th ed.
    p. cm.
  Rev. ed. of: What color is your parachute? job-hunter's workbook. 3rd ed. c2010.
  1. Job hunting. 2. Vocational guidance. 3. Career changes. I. Bolles, Richard Nelson. What color is
your parachute? job-hunter's workbook. II. Title. III. Title: What color is your parachute? job-hunter's
workbook.
  HF5382.7.B643 2012
  650.14—dc23

                              2012037999

ISBN 978-1-60774-497-9

Printed in the United States of America

Skills illustrations by Steven M. Johnson, author of *What the World Needs Now*.

10 9 8 7 6 5 4 3 2

Fourth Edition